T·E·A·C·H
T·H·E·M
THINKING

Mental Menus for
24 Thinking Skills

Robin Fogarty & James Bellanca

IRI/Skylight Training and Publishing, Inc.
Arlington Heights, Illinois

Grateful acknowledgement is made to the following authors and agents for their permission to reprint copyrighted materials:

"The Dinner Party," by Mona Gardner," © 1942 *Saturday Review Magazine*.

"A Whack on the Side of the Head," Copyright © 1983 by Roger Van Oech, Ph.D. Printed with permission from Warner Books, Inc., New York.

SCAMPER brainstorming technique, SCAMPER: *Games For Imagination Development* by Robert F. Eberle, © 1971. Printed with permission of DOK Publishers, East Aurora, New York.

Teach Them Thinking (formerly *Mental Menus*)
Published by IRI/Skylight Training and Publishing, Inc.
2626 S. Clearbrook Dr., Arlington Heights, IL 60005
Phone 800-348-4474, 847-290-6600
FAX 847-290-6609
irisky@xnet.com
http://www.business1.com/iri_sky/

Graphic Design by Jeff Haack
Computer Graphics by Tim Hanrahan

Eighth Printing
© 1986 IRI/Skylight Training and Publishing, Inc.

ISBN 0-932935-03-6
0701D-6-96McN
Item number 600

ACKNOWLEDGMENTS

We'd like to express appreciation to the following special educators for their support on this project:

Dr. Arthur Costa of Sacramento State University in California, who promoted the concept of metacognitive processing as an implicit part of teaching for intelligent behavior.

Dr. Barry Beyer of George Mason University, Virginia, who has promoted the idea of teaching the explicit thinking skills.

Drs. Roger and David Johnson, University of Minnesota, who mentored our thinking about cooperative learning and structured interaction.

Dr. Ronald Brandt, executive editor, ASCD, who has pioneered the resurgence of interest in teaching for, of, and about thinking.

Our special thanks to these individuals for their leadership and influence in teaching for intelligent behavior.

TABLE OF CONTENTS

INTRODUCTION

Questions Teachers Ask About "Mental Menus"

Background and Rationale: Just What Are Mental Menus?

As we become attuned to thinking about our thinking, the analogy between the mind and the computer becomes more and more obvious. Tracking the thought processes and cognitive paths the mind takes in performing thinking skills is much like the flow of operations needed to run a program on the computer. So, too, the menus that are called up on the screen can be likened to the mental menus that are available to our thinking processes, if we consciously think about our thinking, metacognitively.

There is a riddle that states: "Your brain is smarter than you are." In fact, the brain is the most marvelous computer of all. It seeks structure, perceives patterns, recalls associations, and creates relationships. Actually, if we trust our brain to guide us, it *seeks* to channel information for us into some organized format. The brain invites order to help us understand and make sense of the world about us.

For example, as we are faced with a circumstance, our mental menus pop up. Almost intuitively, our brain begins to organize the data by sequencing, prioritizing, grouping, and building analogous relationships. The brain seeks to analyze and synthesize as it evaluates data that lead toward reasoned thought. In fact, the brain "shifts" to the appropriate menus almost on its own.

Our task, then, is one of consciously tracing this phenomena by articulating the processes that occur, to bring them to a level of awareness. Once we become adept at tracing these thought processes, they become familiar patterns for thinking. Then, as we encounter situations, we can consciously select the model or menu for thinking through the task. Thus, our mental menus are essentially the explicit thought patterns we use to solve problems, make decisions, and design creatively. These mental menus become the patterns that we can deliberately call upon as we become critical and creative thinkers.

The purpose of this book is to provide models of those patterns for thinking: our mental menus! Through continued and consistent practice with the models, teachers and students become skillful users of the skills. Over time, applying the thinking skills successfully, by sprinkling them throughout the curriculum content, teachers and students will begin to develop their own versions of mental menus. For you see, this little book is only a beginning. The substantive benefits are found, as always, as we begin to draw upon the richness of our own resources from within; as we adopt and design and experiment on our own. *Teach Them Thinking* is merely the catalyst to ignite the creative capabilities inherent within us to think metacognitively about our creative and critical thought processes.

Content: Just What Skills Are Covered In Mental Menus?

To model the use of concrete examples that clarify abstract concepts, we have selected the computer as the basis of our metaphor: Mental Menus. The menus are elaborations of the cognitive processes that occur as we engage in critical and creative thinking.

To extend the computer metaphor further, the skills are presented within the framework of computer lingo. This glossary of terms illustrates the terminology used throughout the book.

Mental Menus: A Glossary of Terms

| PROGRAM | : the explicit thinking skill |

| PASSWORD | : an acronym of the skill concept |

| DATA BASE | : a definition of the skill |

| LIST | : a list of synonyms for the skill |

| SCAN | : a look at specific examples of the applied skill |

| ENTER | : when to use the skill |

| MENU | : directory of operations used in doing the skill |

| DEBUGGING | : trouble shooting; what to do if . . . |

| VISUAL LAYOUT | : formats, structures, and patterns to use with the skill |

| FILE | : a specific example of a classroom application of the skill |

| INDEX | : a list of suggested subject area applications for practice |

THE EXPLICIT SKILLS

Twenty-four explicit skills are extensively developed in *Teach Them Thinking*. These skills are divided into critical thinking and creative thinking skills. The authors differentiate between this duality of skill categories in this way.

Critical Thinking Skills require analytic, evaluative processing while Creative Thinking Skills dictate synthesis and a generative model of thinking. However,

a word of caution is warranted here. Although we have purposefully separated the skills, in reality they are often used almost simultaneously as we process an idea. So the division is somewhat artificial as we consider a more holistic approach to problem solving, decision making, and creativity.

With that thought in mind, the specific skills illustrated within this framework are outlined here:

CRITICAL THINKING SKILLS:

1. Attributing — TRAITS
2. Comparing And Contrasting — SAD
3. Classifying — CLUE
4. Sequencing — SORT
5. Prioritizing — RANK
6. Drawing Conclusions — DRAW
7. Determining Cause And Effect — CHAINS
8. Analyzing For Bias — BIAS
9. Analyzing For Assumption — ASSUME
10. Solving Analogies — SOLVE
11. Evaluating — RATE
12. Decision Making — JUDGE

CREATIVE THINKING SKILLS:

1. Brainstorming — THINK
2. Visualizing — IMAGES
3. Personifying — LIVE
4. Inventing — SCAMPER
5. Associating Relationships — RELATE
6. Inferring — INFER
7. Generalizing — RULE
8. Predicting — BET
9. Hypothesizing — THEORY
10. Making Analogies — MAKE
11. Dealing With Ambiguity And Paradox — DUAL
12. Problem Solving — IDEAS

THE CLUSTER CURRICULUM:

The listings are not intended to suggest a hierarchial structure, although certain skills do seem to logically fall into a cluster of sorts. For instance, attributing must precede skills such as comparing and contrasting and

classification since these latter skills are ascertained through determining attributes. Therefore, attributing is a target or foundation skill for other thinking skills. The diagram illustrates suggested skill clusters.

THE CLUSTER CURRICULUM

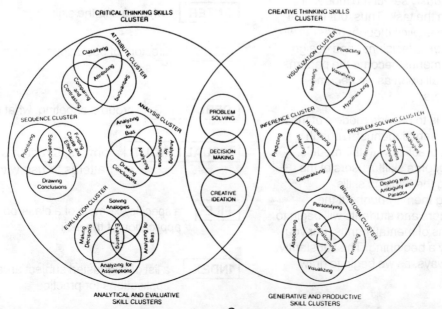

CRITICAL THINKING SKILLS CLUSTER

CREATIVE THINKING SKILLS CLUSTER

ANALYTICAL AND EVALUATIVE SKILL CLUSTERS

GENERATIVE AND PRODUCTIVE SKILL CLUSTERS

THE CLUSTER CURRICULUM

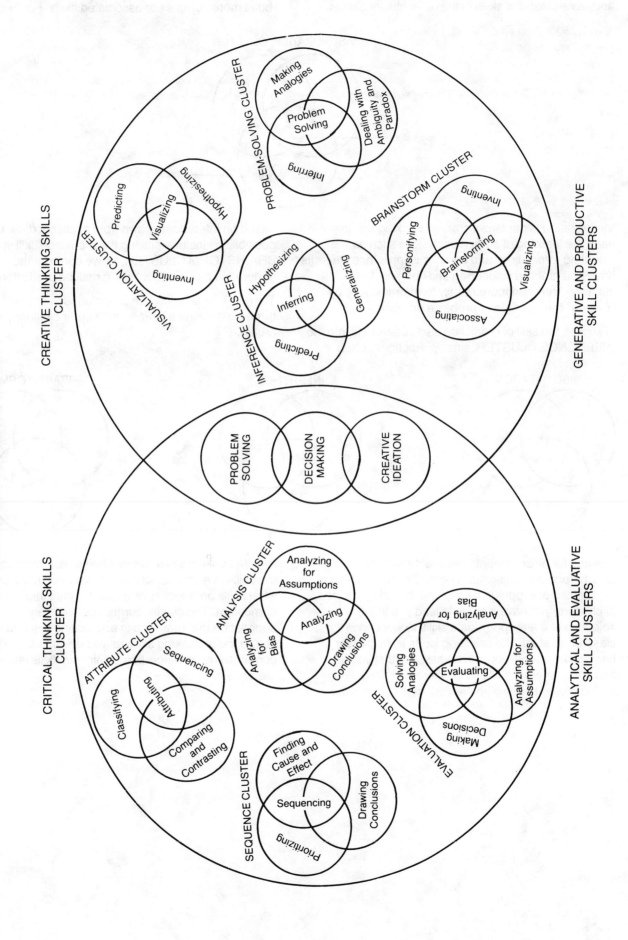

CREATIVE THINKING SKILLS CLUSTER

PROBLEM-SOLVING CLUSTER

Making Analogies

Problem Solving

Dealing with Ambiguity and Paradox

Inferring

VISUALIZATION CLUSTER

Predicting

Visualizing

Hypothesizing

Inventing

INFERENCE CLUSTER

Hypothesizing

Inferring

Generalizing

Predicting

BRAINSTORM CLUSTER

Inventing

Personifying

Brainstorming

Visualizing

Associating

GENERATIVE AND PRODUCTIVE SKILL CLUSTERS

PROBLEM SOLVING

DECISION MAKING

CREATIVE IDEATION

CRITICAL THINKING SKILLS CLUSTER

ATTRIBUTE CLUSTER

Sequencing

Classifying

Attributing

Comparing and Contrasting

ANALYSIS CLUSTER

Analyzing for Assumptions

Analyzing for Bias

Analyzing

Drawing Conclusions

EVALUATION CLUSTER

Analyzing for Bias

Solving Analogies

Evaluating

Analyzing for Assumptions

Making Decisions

SEQUENCE CLUSTER

Finding Cause and Effect

Sequencing

Drawing Conclusions

Prioritizing

ANALYTICAL AND EVALUATIVE SKILL CLUSTERS

Each skill cluster includes a target skill as the center and several related skills in the outer cluster circles.

The target skill provides the foundation upon which to build more complex or associated skills. For example:

VISUALIZATION CLUSTER

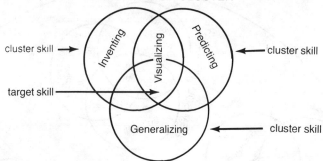

cluster skill → Inventing Visualizing Predicting ← cluster skill

target skill → Generalizing ← cluster skill

Visualization is the *target* creative thinking skill that will ease the learning of outer cluster skills such as inventing, predicting, and hypothesizing. Once students have had practice visualizing and imaging, for instance, they can more readily form predictions by "seeing" the possible or probable outcomes.

However, the skill of prediction also seems to fit into the INFERENCE CLUSTER, since predicting is often based on inferences drawn from available data. Other possibilities include placing the prediction skill in a BRAINSTORM CLUSTER, as we consider the generative process involved in making predictions.

Therefore, predicting can be included in any one of the three clusters, in all three, or in other clusters you create.

VISUALIZATION

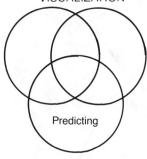

Predicting

INFERENCE

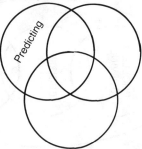

Predicting

BRAINSTORM

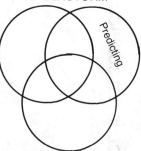

Predicting

The cluster arrangements are intentionally presented as arbitrary, permitting fluid constructs of skill clusters as deemed appropriate by you. Yet, by using the idea of clusters, you have a guide to lead you in the selection of a few appropriate skills to work on in the classroom. Much like selecting foods from the four basic food groups, you can be assured that you are sampling different skills from different clusters and giving students a "well-balanced" curriculum in the area of thinking skills, without being mandated to use the skills in a structured order. Again, you must decide what skills are most appropriate to "plug into" your curriculum. The cluster curriculum is merely a suggestion that may help in articulating a scope and sequence of thinking skills as you develop a comprehensive integration of thinking skills into your classroom.

SKILL INTRODUCTION:

Just How Do I Introduce Thinking Skills To My Class?

THINKING IS

like the ability to move or
perform as a ballerina
or athlete . . . left to our
own devices, the body does
not move with style and grace
. . . so too, left to our
own devices, the human
intellect does not function
very well . . . We must
educate for intelligent
performance . . . with
rehearsal, practice, and coaching.

A thinking skill is just that — a skill — and like any skill it requires explicit instruction to fully develop the inherent intellectual talent. To introduce an explicit thinking skill, the skill itself becomes the focus of the lesson. The content used to develop the lesson is merely a vehicle to present the skill. That content should be familiar to the students. Once the skill has been taught explicitly, it can be applied with new content as students interact to process the material.

For example, in the introductory skill lesson on classification, the science content of the states of matter is somewhat familiar to intermediate students. Therefore, we can focus the objective on the *skill* of classification. Once students have had ample opportunities to practice the skill, classification can be applied to new learning.

In short, the explicit skill lesson highlights the skill itself. This introductory lesson helps bring the skill to a conscious level so that students become acutely aware of the processing involved.

Within the explicit instruction, the introductory lesson includes:

- a stated objective
- a definition of terms
- examples of the applied skill
- informational content
- modeling
- guided practice with the skill
- independent practice
- transfer applications
- metacognitive processing

A sample lesson outlines the format used to develop each thinking skill.

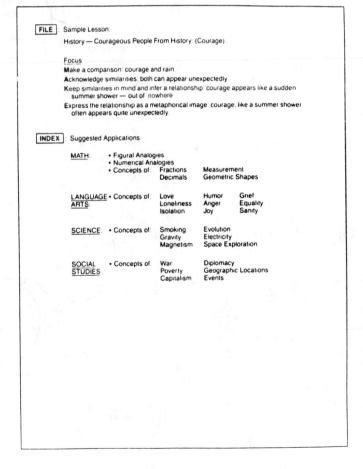

MAKING ANALOGIES

[X] Creative Thinking   [ ] Critical Thinking

PROGRAM : Skill: Making Analogies   **PASSWORD** : Acronym: **MAKE**

DATA BASE : Definition: Creating metaphors to visualize an idea.

LIST : Synonyms: metaphors, similes

SCAN : Examples: Reasoning by analogy to make abstract concept more concrete; rage as thunder; sun as love.

ENTER : When to use:
— to grasp abstract concepts
— to present ideas in unique ways
— to communicate a complex thought

MENU : How to use:
Make a comparison of two unlike things.
Acknowledge the similarities.
Keep the similarities in mind and *infer* a relationship.
Express the relationship as a metaphorical image.

DEBUGGING : What to do if:
— can't find similarities; keep brainstorming using all your senses or change comparison.

VISUAL LAYOUT : Patterns: Thought Trees
_____ is like _____ because both _____.

FILE : Sample Lesson:
History — Courageous People From History. (Courage)

Focus
Make a comparison: courage and rain.
Acknowledge similarities: both can appear unexpectedly.
Keep similarities in mind and infer a relationship: courage appears like a sudden summer shower — out of nowhere.
Express the relationship as a metaphorical image: courage, like a summer shower often appears quite unexpectedly.

INDEX : Suggested Applications:

MATH:	• Figural Analogies			
	• Numerical Analogies			
	• Concepts of:	Fractions	Measurement	
		Decimals	Geometric Shapes	
LANGUAGE ARTS:	• Concepts of:	Love	Humor	Grief
		Loneliness	Anger	Equality
		Isolation	Joy	Sanity
SCIENCE:	• Concepts of:	Smoking	Evolution	
		Gravity	Electricity	
		Magnetism	Space Exploration	
SOCIAL STUDIES:	• Concepts of:	War	Diplomacy	
		Poverty	Geographic Locations	
		Capitalism	Events	

USING AN INDUCTIVE OR DEDUCTIVE STRATEGY:

Another consideration is which strategy to use to introduce the explicit thinking skill: an inductive strategy or a deductive strategy.

Inductive lesson design is based on the concept of inquiry. Using the inductive strategy, specific bits of information are assembled and a generalization results. Inductive techniques, much like a detective accumulating clues, require seeing patterns and making associations from scattered information and generating a statement that encompasses the suggested results. Students experiment and reflect, apply and review the learning when using an inductive method.

Inductive strategies are appropriate for most classroom lessons since the bulk of our 'learning in life' is obtained inductively. Inductive strategies however, require more skilled teaching and more effective classroom management.

On the other hand, a deductive strategy can be useful in some situations. In the deductive method, a general statement is outlined and demonstrated and then information is processed to determine if it "fits the rule." Doctors use deductive techniques when diagnosing an illness. They try to match the symptoms with known profiles of specific diseases. In essence, they begin with a broad definition and slot the specific facts to the known patterns until they find the "perfect fit." Thus, they can make the diagnosis, treatment, and prognosis.

To use deductive techniques in the classroom, the teacher explains and demonstrates and then has the students apply the content to the defined structure. In the last stages, the students reflect on the learning.

Deductive strategies are most effective when the skill is especially difficult or complex and/or when the learners are novices or lacking in similar experiences. For example, when introducing the skill of inventing which includes *nine* separate strategies, it is best to plan a deductive lesson in which you first, *explain* fully the nine strategies, *demonstrate* their use and then have students *apply* the new information.

Explict Skill Instruction

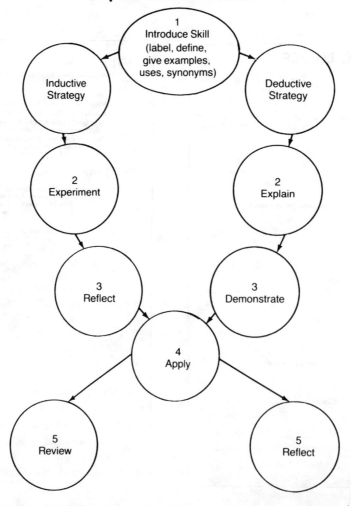

The diagram above illustrates the two methods available to introduce a thinking skill.

Skill: CLASSIFICATION

<table>
<tr><td>An Inductive Lesson</td><td>A Deductive Lesson</td></tr>
</table>

① Introduce the skill
(label, define, give examples,
uses, and synonyms)

② Provide students with a list of words from the science chapter. Ask them to group the words in some way. Allow time for processing of their activity, facilitating as necessary.

② Explain the concept of classification using a list of words from the science chapter. Proceed systematically through the list and find classification labels that are appropriate.

③ Guide students to reflect on the classification they made. Display the groupings and discuss the variations. Elicit rules for classifying from students.

③ Label the groups and classify the words according to those labels. Explain why you place items in particular groups as you proceed.

④ Have students apply the learning about classification in a social studies or reading lesson.

⑤ Review the skill of classification and elicit other applications of the skill.

⑤ Guide students to reflect on the classifications they made and discuss *how* we classify things.

EXTENDING THE SKILL LESSONS:

Just How Do I Go About Creating And Generating Menus In The Classroom?

There appear to be two distinct steps necessary to begin creating and generating menus in the classroom. The first step involves teacher readiness, while the second step concerns guiding students in the development of thinking skills. The two steps in this process are explained here.

How teachers learn the Explicit Thinking Skill:

After using the formats and ideas set forth in *Teach Them Thinking*, you will want to develop some menus on your own. There is no secret recipe! To begin to articulate the thought patterns used in a thinking skill, make a mental list of what you do when you think critically or creatively. Track your thoughts and be aware of the components of the process.

A good way to start is to take a moment the next time you have an unexpected "challenge". For example, consciously think about your thinking as you figure out what to do when you have a flat tire, or your son loses the car keys, or you're out of mayonnaise and the tuna fish is already in the bowl. How do you decide whether or not to take the promotion even though it means moving to another part of the country? Track your thinking processes. How do you go about dealing with the challenges and occurrences that arise in life?

Once you consciously trace your thought processes in this fashion, you are on your way to developing your own mental menus. For example, delineate your method for handling an avalanche of newly dictated grading policies. How do you organize the unfamiliar guidelines? How do you connect them to your "old" ways? How do you go about assimilating them into a manageable manner for implementation? Answering these kinds of questions will lead you into the metacognitive processing necessary to the development of Mental Menus. It brings to an awareness level the thinking that makes explicit the very patterns for thinking that you already use.

How students learn the Explicit Thinking Skills:

Skilled thinkers think about their thinking. To help all students become skillful thinkers who can track their own thinking, the "paired partners" strategy provides a possible beginning.

In "paired partners" the students take turns articulating the steps they use in solving a problem. Just by asking for a verbal recitation of the process, students are forced to track their thinking. And, again, with many practices they become skilled at doing this. In no time at all, the teacher will be able to elicit Mental Menus from the students as new thinking skills are introduced.

MAKING MENUS IN THE CLASSROOM:

STEP 1: | **PROGRAM** | : Skill:

Select a thinking skill.

STEP 2: | **DATA BASE** | : Definition:

Develop a definition of the skill with the students using their own wording.

STEP 3: | **LIST** | : Synonyms:

Elicit synonyms from the students.

STEP 4: | **SCAN** | : Examples:

Cite a concrete example of an application of the skill. Have students think of other applications.

STEP 5: | **ENTER** | : **When to use:**

List appropriate instances in which the skill is used.

STEP 6: | **MENU** | : **How to use:**

Outline the operations used to perform the skill. Then, use a word symbolic of the skill and rewrite the operations in the form of an acronym.

STEP 7: Develop an acronym as a memory aid *after* you track the necessary operations in Step 6. (PASSWORD)

STEP 8: | **DEBUGGING** | : **What to do if:**

Explore possible snags in performing the skill and decide on possible alternatives that allow you to proceed.

STEP 9: | **VISUAL LAYOUT** | : Patterns:

List graphic organizers that provide an aid in using the skill.

STEP 10: | **FILE** | : Sample Lesson:

Develop a sample skill lesson using subject area content.

STEP 11: | **INDEX** | : Suggested Applications:

Think of further applications in other subject area content: plug the skill into relevant topics.

STEP 7: | **PASSWORD** | : Acronym:

Develop an acronym as a memory aid *after* you track the necessary operations in Step 6.

APPLICATION:

Just How Do I Use These Skills In My Classroom?

Once the explicit thinking skill has been introduced, using the skill in the normal course of lessons follows. Learners need practice, rehearsal, and coaching with a new skill.

Practice and rehearsal can be achieved by "bridging" the skill into content areas. For example, the skill of classification can be used with science units, social studies concepts, spelling words, or in grouping the stories in a reading unit.

Frequent application of the skill, using the content *already* included in the curriculum, is the most effective application of the thinking skills. In this way, thinking skills do not become an "add-on" to the curriculum, but merely strategies to help students process the material already slotted for study.

With practice, you will find many opportunities to "plug in" thinking skills. For example, after teaching the skill of analysis by attributing, you can "plug in" the attribute web as you go about your regularly scheduled lessons.

As you work with a piece of *literature*, you can ask students to use the attribute web to analyze the leading character. During the *social studies* lessons, students can develop attribute webs of the various geographic regions as they analyze the material presented in the text. A *math* unit on fractions can be introduced with the attribute web as a diagnostic strategy to determine the prior knowledge of students. An additional application of the skill of attributing can be bridged into the *science* lesson. Student webs can be used to analyze the attributes of mammals as you study the biology unit. The webs below suggest the range of applications for this one skill.

SKILL: ATTRIBUTING
TRANSFER LESSONS
(Practice, practice, practice)

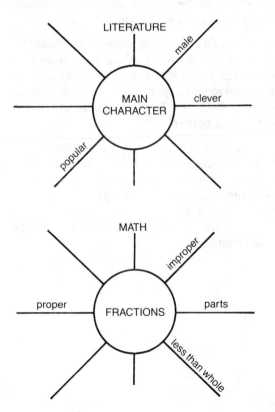

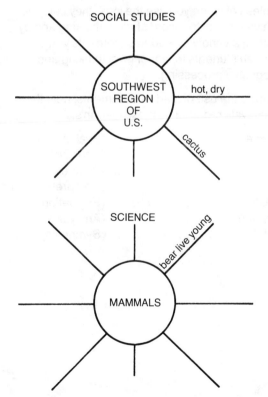

To vary the application of the analysis attribute web, the whole class can develop a web or students can work in small groups to produce a finished web using the same target concept. Also, the jigsaw puzzle model can be used in which each small group is assigned a "piece" of the total "picture." For instance, in social studies, five groups would work on five webs: the Southwest, Northwest, Midwest, South, and

Northeast. Then the five webs are presented to the class and the jigsaw puzzle "picture" takes form.

As teachers provide lots of practice with a skill, students will begin to transfer these mental patterns into other relevant situations as they become more skillful thinkers.

Accompanying the continuous and consistent practices with the skills, immediate, specific feedback is required, as well as frequent opportunities for metacognitive processing of the skill applications.

The Thinking Log and thoughtful discussions using higher-level questioning can lead students comfortably into the metacognitive areas of thinking about their thinking.

The Thinking Log can be used effectively at various spots throughout a lesson. To spark kids interest, review past learning or to get them to focus on the concept, you can have them make a log entry *before* the lesson actually begins.

To capture spontaneous student reactions, you might have them go to their logs *immediately following* the processing activity. This need only take a minute or two and can be an effective "sponge" activity during *transition* times.

Another natural opportunity for log entries is as a closure task *after* the lesson has been completed. This gives students a moment to reflect on the "big idea" presented during the lesson.

Regardless of when you use the logs, they can become a viable tool to record student thinking and by suggesting a variety of lead-in statements you can gently push students to higher-level thinking and metacognitive processing.

To illustrate the use of lead-in statements, note the thinking levels required by these lead-in's:

I believe	(Evaluation)
I wonder	(Analysis)
Suppose	(Synthesis)
I think	(Comprehension &?)
I question	(Evaluation)
Comparing	(Analysis)
What if	(Synthesis)

Students may also be lead toward visual processing in the log. By suggesting that they diagram or graph or "map" their perceptions of an idea, students begin to use graphic patterns to chart their thinking.

If opportunities are given, students will learn to use their log as yet another method for tracking their thinking.

CONCLUSION: What Do I Do Now?

Now, select a Mental Menu most generic to your content . . . and begin there. Don't be in a hurry to bombard the students with *lots* of skills. Get one going first. Do it right! Take the necessary time to introduce it explicitly and give ample practice applications with the skill. Process it! Plug it into your lessons until it becomes an automatic pattern for thinking with the students.

Teaching an explicit thinking skill begins with a thorough introduction of the components of the skill. But mastery of the skill requires lots of short, busy practices at first, followed by a variety of opportunities to apply the new skill to meaningful situations.

Much like the child who learns to swim, the student must be led gently into skillful thinking. Each component of the skill is tackled separately and eventually the actions are strung together until the body moves easily through the water. Teaching for skillful thinking follows the same pattern.

A reasonable approach to new things is always the wisest. We consider a thorough development of two or three skills a year a reasonable goal. If these two or three skills are elaborated and integrated properly, students will have a good start toward becoming productive problem solvers, mindful decision makers, and creative thinkers.

Teaching For Mastery Of A Thinking Skill

Introduction of Skill:
Familiar Content

> Practice
> Practice
> Practice

Transfer of Skill:
One Content Area

> Practice
> Practice
> Practice

Transfer of Skill:
New Content Area

> Practice
> Practice
> Practice

Transfer of Skill:
Yet Another Content Area

> Practice
> Practice
> Practice

Apply Skill On Own:
Pattern For Thinking

> Use
> Use
> Use

What Does The School or District Do Next?

Without expanding on a complete curriculum design here, the authors do suggest that teachers within a building, grade level, or department, or teachers across grade levels and disciplines will want to begin to articulate with each other concerning an implementation plan for introducing thinking skills in the curriculum. Eventually, a scope and sequence needs to be developed to provide comprehensive coverage of the skills for the student. But, for now, just begin within your classroom. Experiment and expand as you feel ready. Start on the pattern to skillful thinking, now.

Thinking About You . . .
Robin & Jim

CRITICAL THINKING SKILLS

ATTRIBUTING

T une in; focus

R un with it; brainstorm

A ssociate ideas; piggy-back

I mage the concept or item; define it

T est the attributes

S elect the critical attributes

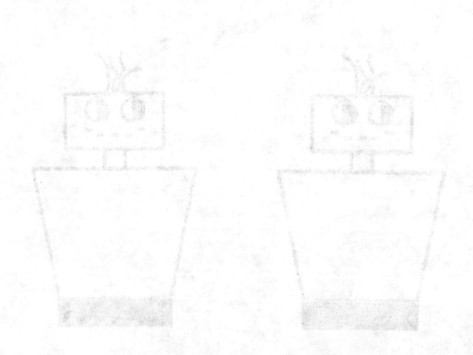

ATTRIBUTING

☐ Creative Thinking   ☒ Critical Thinking

PROGRAM : Skill: Attributing

PASSWORD : Acronym: **TRAITS**

DATA BASE : Definition: Analyze characteristics, qualities, elements, or traits of a concept or item.

LIST : Synonyms: characteristics, traits, likenesses

SCAN : Examples: Attributes of mammals; attributes of courage

ENTER : When to use:
— to define concept or item
— to distinguish between two similar concepts or items
— to clarify concept in own terms

MENU : How to use:

Tune in; focus

Run with it; brainstorm

Associate ideas; piggy-back

Image the concept or item; define it

Test the attributes with a specific example

Select the critical attributes necessary to define concept or item

DEBUGGING : What to do if:
— cannot separate it from similar concept; find specific example to use as model; use references or resource material.
— cannot select critical attributes; keep all.
— cannot think of specific example to test with; get help from someone or continue to add attributes until more clearly defined.

VISUAL LAYOUT : Patterns: Attribute Web
List
Concept Map

FILE : Sample Lesson:

Language Arts: Literature — A Mystery

Tune in — think of a mystery on TV or a book

Run with it — clues, suspense, problem-solution, hero (associate idea of characters)

Associate — hero   victim   suspects

Image — clues lead to climax — several possibilities

Test — specific mystery — did it have all these attributes?

Select — problem, hero, victim, suspects, clues, suspense; (no victim, therefore eliminate from final list of attributes, i.e. — can have mystery without victim.)

INDEX : Suggested Applications:

MATH:
- Metric System
- Graphs
- Word Problems

LANGUAGE ARTS:
- Paragraph
- Character Analysis

SCIENCE:
- UFO's
- Nutritious Foods
- Force

SOCIAL STUDIES:
- Leaders
- War
- Geographic Location

COMPARING AND CONTRASTING

SEE SIMILARITIES

ATTRIBUTE

DELINEATE DIFFERENCES

COMPARING AND CONTRASTING

☐ Creative Thinking   ☒ Critical Thinking

PROGRAM : Skill: Comparing/Contrasting   **PASSWORD** : Acronym: **SAD**

DATA BASE : Definition: Finding similarities and differences by attributing

LIST : Synonyms: similarities and differences, matching

SCAN : Example: Comparing and contrasting automobiles

ENTER : <u>When to use</u>: Comparing and contrasting when:
— two or more possibilities occur
— making a decision or choice

MENU : <u>How to use</u>:
See similarities
Attribute
Delineate differences

DEBUGGING : <u>What to do if</u>:
— similar but a little different, place in both circles of the Venn and qualify or place in one circle of the Venn and qualify.
— having trouble finding similarities and differences; research; get more data.

VISUAL LAYOUT : Patterns: Venn Diagrams
Columns

COMPARING AND CONTRASTING

FILE : Sample Lesson:

American History: Protest — Colonists protest and protest today
nuclear power (characteristics of protest: violent/non-violent)

Sense similarities by comparing:

Colonists	Today's Citizens
posted notices	notices in magazines, etc.
rallied people	seek supporters
public speeches	public service messages
pamphlets	pamphlets
appealed to government authorities	appealed to government authorities

Attribute

Delineate differences by contrasting:

Colonists	Today's Citizens
used violence	non-violence
boycotted	picket
rioted	bumper stickers
fought	TV/radio/newspapers major use of media

Then: Check for Consistency:
— could change rallied people or sought supporters so more consistent

Statement of Findings: While the colonists and today's citizenry both use public notices, supporters, public speeches, pamphlets, and appeals to government authorities to protest actions they oppose, there are also distinguishing differences in their methods. The colonists were more inclined to use physical force with riots and fighting, whereas today's citizens use the media and pickets in actions that are less violent in nature.

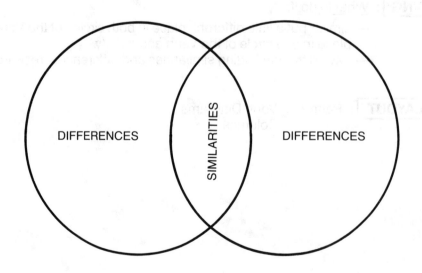

INDEX : Suggested Applications:

MATH:
- Triangles and Squares
- Fractions and Decimals
- Distributive Law and Commutative Law

LANGUAGE
ARTS:
- Fact and Fiction
- Characters: Tom Sawyer and Huck Finn
- Styles of Hemingway and Fitzgerald

SCIENCE:
- Acids and Bases
- Life Cycles of Plants and Animals
- Magnetic and Non-Magnetic Objects

SOCIAL
STUDIES:
- Cities and Rural Communities
- Free Enterprise and Communism
- Northern and Southern Views on Desegregation

CLASSIFYING

Collect data

Label group

Use pattern

Evaluate pattern

CLASSIFYING

☐ Creative Thinking   ☒ Critical Thinking

PROGRAM : Skill: Classifying   **PASSWORD** : Acronym: **CLUE**

DATA BASE : Definition: To sort into groups on the basis of common characteristics (attributes).

LIST : Synonyms: Groups, sets, sorting, categorizing

SCAN : Examples: Grouping rocks, books, animal species

ENTER : When to use:
  — data unorganized
  — lot of data

MENU : How to use:

  Collect data
  Label group
  Use pattern
  Evaluate pattern

DEBUGGING : What to do if:
  — items don't fit; label miscellaneous.
  — data in category vary; sub-group or regroup.
  — item fits more than one, reclassify with new broader or more focused labels.
  — begin to run out of items for one label; switch to another.

VISUAL LAYOUT : Patterns: Venn Diagram
                                   Charts
                                   Matrix
                                   Morphological Grid

FILE : Sample Lesson:

Science — Chemistry: Liquid, Solid, Gas (Physical States of Matter)

Collect Data:
wood	soft drink	milk
Coffee cup	air	iced tea
paint	muddy water	ice
sugar cube	carbon dioxide	mercury
pure table salt	T-bone steak	blood
sea water	cough syrup	popcorn

Label similar items in a group:

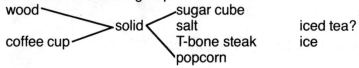

wood
coffee cup → solid → sugar cube, salt, T-bone steak, popcorn   iced tea? ice

Use pattern to add others:

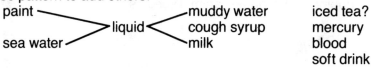

paint
sea water → liquid → muddy water, cough syrup, milk   iced tea? mercury blood soft drink

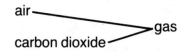

air
carbon dioxide → gas

Evaluate pattern:

Question: where iced tea fits — solid or liquid, decide to keep it in <u>both</u> categories.
Evaluation: classifications: ok; double check for gases — only 2.

INDEX : Suggested Applications:

<u>MATH</u>:
- Types of Triangles
- Types of Graphs
- Prime Numbers

<u>LANGUAGE ARTS</u>:
- Dewey Decimal System
- Tall Tales, Myths, Fables
- Homonyms, Synonyms, Antonyms

<u>SCIENCE</u>:
- Trees: Coniferous/Deciduous
- Rocks: Sedimentary, Metamorphic, Igneous
- Heterogeneous/Homogeneous Matter

<u>SOCIAL STUDIES</u>:
- Causes of Civil War: Economic, Political, Social
- Native Americans
- Political Ideologies

SEQUENCING

S can for subtle differences

O rder

R eadjust

T est

SEQUENCING

☐ Creative Thinking  ☒ Critical Thinking

PROGRAM : Skill: Sequencing

PASSWORD : Acronym: **SORT**

DATA BASE : Definition: Arranging items in order by distinguishing attributes; size, time, color.

LIST : Synonyms: ordering, flow charting, serializing

SCAN : Examples: Historical time lines, sequencing steps to act on, listing order

ENTER : When to use:
— lot of data
— need steps to follow
— want to distinguish subtle differences
— want to organize

MENU : How to use:
Scan for similarities and differences
Order
Readjust
Test

DEBUGGING : What to do if:
— something seems out of order; readjust and insert where it belongs.
— too much data; pre-sort into smaller segments; sequence each segment, then assemble total picture.
— unsure of placement in ordering criteria, temporarily place — readjust as needed as you progress.

VISUAL LAYOUT : Patterns: Time Lines
Flow Charts
Plot Line

FILE : Sample Lesson:

Language Arts: Organizing a Long-Term Project
(How to Write a Research Paper)

Scan facts: Books and Reference Material
Topic
Bibliography
Outline
Paper

Order: (1) Select topic, get reference and materials together
(2) Outline ideas
(3) Make notes; organize according to outline
(4) Write 1st draft
(5) Revise and reorder as needed for final draft

Readjust: (6) Make bibliography

Test: (7) Type

INDEX : Suggested Applications:

MATH: • Flow Chart — Computer Program
• Ordering Questions in Problem Solving
• Geometric Patterns

LANGUAGE • Biographical Time Line of Tolstoy
ARTS: • Verbal Sequences: (ie: tepid, warm, hot, boiling)
• Plot Line of a Mystery

SCIENCE: • Metamorphosis of a Butterfly
• Development of a Photograph
• Stages of an Atomic Reaction

PRIORITIZING

R EVIEW ALL ITEMS

A DAPT CRITERIA

N OTE TOP AND BOTTOM ITEMS

K EY IN ON 'MIDDLE' OF LIST

PRIORITIZING

☐ Creative Thinking   [X] Critical Thinking

PROGRAM : Skill: Prioritizing   **PASSWORD** : Acronym: **RANK**

DATA BASE : Definition: Rank ordering according to determined value.

LIST : Synonyms: ranking, ordering, selecting

SCAN : Examples: Homework — order of assignments or packing for a trip — selecting most important items

ENTER : When to use:
— planning
— evaluating
— selecting options
— deciding

MENU : How to use:

Review all items

Adapt criteria: time, value, deadline, energy, mood, goal

Note top items and bottom items on list

Key in on 'middle' of list

DEBUGGING : What to do if:
— items seem equal; review criteria — choose one
— unsure of one item; rank it 'down' if unsure, probably not a priority

VISUAL LAYOUT : Patterns: List
                              Rank Ladder
                              Criteria Matrix

FILE : Sample Lesson:

Language Arts: Composition

Rank the following according to their importance to writing:
1. quality of content
2. grammar
3. subject
4. format (poetry, novel, etc.)
5. emotional appeal
6. spelling
7. knowledge
8. length
9. introduction
10. style
11. conclusion
12. title

Review items; number 1-12 on paper.

Adapt criteria: <u>Goal:</u> To communicate one's ideas through writing.

Note top and bottom of list:

<u>TOP</u>	<u>BOTTOM</u>
(1) content	(10) knowledge
(2) title	(11) length
(3) emotional appeal	(12) spelling

Key in on 'middle':

(4) introduction	(7) format
(5) style	(8) conclusion
(6) subject	(9) grammar

(Discuss why!)

INDEX : Suggested Applications:

<u>MATH</u>:
- Stock Market
- Topics of Relevance (Chapters in Book)
- Consumer Education: "Best Buy" in Product Line

<u>LANGUAGE</u>
<u>ARTS</u>:
- Selecting a Research Topic
- Best Commercials on T.V.
- Authors Studied

<u>SCIENCE</u>:
- Funding Areas for Medical Research
- Importance of Inventions (List)
- Components of "Wellness" (Health)

<u>SOCIAL</u>
<u>STUDIES</u>:
- Attributes for Presidential Candidate
- Funding for Federal Programs
- Occupations for Societal Benefits

DRAWING CONCLUSIONS

D RAW TOGETHER

R EORDER IN LOGICAL SEQUENCE

A NALYZE PATTERNS

W RITE YOUR CONCLUSION

DRAWING CONCLUSIONS

☐ Creative Thinking   ☒ Critical Thinking

PROGRAM : Skill: Drawing Conclusions   **PASSWORD** : Acronym: **DRAW**

DATA BASE : Definition: Analyzing facts and hypothesizing a logical outcome based on the evidence.

LIST : Synonyms: deduce, determine

SCAN : Examples: Drawing conclusions in a mystery, drawing conclusions about engine failure in your car

ENTER : When to use:
— anticipating outcomes
— predicting outcomes
— reconstructing an incident

MENU : How to use:

Draw together all the facts.
Reorder in logical sequence or groups beginning with groups of clues that fit together.
Analyze patterns; assemble a picture in your mind of the events.
Write your conclusion, supporting it with the evidence.

DEBUGGING : What to do if:
— some clues don't make sense, put them aside for the time being, then go back.
— several conclusions evolve; use both as hypotheses for further checking; choose best and investigate more.

VISUAL LAYOUT : Patterns: Flow Chart
                                             Sequencing Chart
                                             Venn Diagram

FILE : Sample Lessons:

Language Arts: Drawing Conclusions from Novels
                (*The Old Man And The Sea* — Hemingway)

After reading Hemingway's novel:

Draw together facts about old man and the boy. (i.e.: persistent, kind, old, caring,
    wise, hungry)

Reorder the data in logical sequence or groups.

Analyze patterns; assemble a picture of each in your mind.

Write a description of each character by drawing conclusions from the facts in the reading.

INDEX : Suggested Applications:

MATH: • Geometry Theorems
               • Story Problems

LANGUAGE • Mystery Novels
ARTS: • Science Fiction
               • Tales of the Unknown

SCIENCE: • Lab Experiments
               • Research

SOCIAL   • Assessing Outcomes of an Incident
STUDIES: • Trend Analysis

DETERMINING CAUSE AND EFFECT

C HOOSE A SITUATION

H AVE POSSIBLE OUTCOMES IN MIND

A DVANCE ONE IDEA

I NDICATE THE 'CHAIN OF EVENTS'

N OTE THE CAUSE/EFFECT RELATIONSHIP OR

S TART AT OUTCOME AND WORK BACKWARD

DETERMINING CAUSE AND EFFECT

☐ Creative Thinking [X] Critical Thinking

PROGRAM : Skill: Determining Cause and Effect   **PASSWORD** : Acronym: **CHAINS**

DATA BASE : Definition: To determine cause and effect relationships.

LIST : Synonyms: action — consequence; catalyst — outcome; chain — reaction concept;
cause — result

SCAN : Examples: Drop match in woods; ignites leaves; spreads to trees ⟶ forest fire [loss of
natural resource results in wood and by-products price increase.]

i.e. match causes effect of forest fire ⟶ which causes prices to rise on
wood products.

ENTER : When to use:

— planning a course of action; options
— analyzing the cause of a particular consequence, result or effect

MENU : How to use:

Choose a situation
Have possible outcomes in mind
Advance one idea
Indicate the 'chain of events'
Note the cause/effect relationship or
Start at outcome and work backward

DEBUGGING : What to do if:

— cannot decide on outcome; work through several probable outcomes;
prepare for both.
— tracing backward and have several possible causes; check each one further to
clarify or narrow to most probable cause.

VISUAL LAYOUT : Patterns: Cause-Effect Chain
                              Flow Chart

FILE : Sample Lesson:

Earth Science: Effects of Weather

Record March snowfalls have left heavy coverage on the ground. What effects can be anticipated in the spring? Why? What can farmers do to prepare? Explain.

Choose situation: heavy snows

Have outcomes in mind: quick thaw, slow thaw

Advance one idea: quick thaw

Indicate chain of events: quick thaw ⟶ floods ⟶ wet ground ⟶ late planting ⟶ late crops ⟶ farmers have financial problems

Note cause/effect relationship: heavy March snow ⟶ thaw ⟶ flood ⟶ or

Start at end: financial problems ⟶ late crop ⟶ flood ⟶ snow

INDEX : Suggested Applications:

MATH: • Statistics
               • Probabilities
               • Stock Market
               • Logic — If . . . then

LANGUAGE   • Analyzing Events in a Story
ARTS: • Constructing Alternate Plots and Outcomes

SCIENCE: • Chemical Reactions
               • Environmental Issues
               • Physics — Action/Reaction

SOCIAL   • Economics
STUDIES   • Current Events (political)
               • History — What if . . .
               • Government — Law

ANALYZING FOR BIAS

Be aware of point of view

Indicate bias clues

   Exaggeration

   Overgeneralization

   Imbalance

   Opinion as fact

   Charged words

Account for possible bias

State opinion

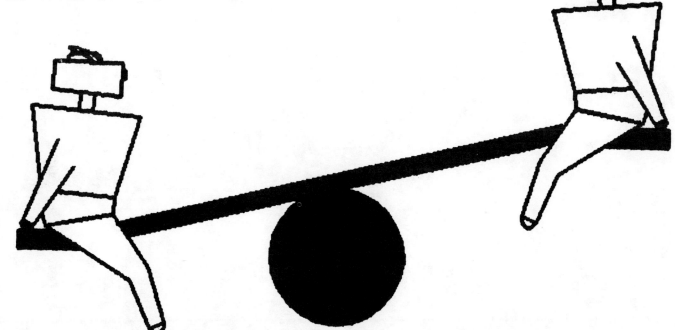

ANALYZING FOR BIAS

☐ Creative Thinking  ☒ Critical Thinking

PROGRAM : Skill: Analyzing for Bias   **PASSWORD** : Acronym: **BIAS**

DATA BASE : Definition: Examining material for point of view and possible misrepresentation.

LIST : Synonyms: prejudiced, bigoted, slanted

SCAN : Example: Advertising

ENTER : When to use:
— reading, listening, and acting as a critical thinker with advertising, political speaker, etc.

MENU : How to use:
Be aware of point of view
Indicate spottings of bias clues (**EOIOC**):
    Exaggeration
    Overgeneralization
    Imbalance
    Opinion as fact
    Charged words
Account for possible bias by citing proofs
State opinion based on 'reasoned judgment'

DEBUGGING : What to do if:
— not sure of point-of-view; go on; try to discover.
— cannot find bias clues explicitly; articulate <u>feeling</u>, then pinpoint <u>why</u> you feel that way, re-examine data.

VISUAL LAYOUT : Patterns: Thought Trees
Venn Diagram

FILE : Sample Lesson:

History: Presidential Profile

(Analysis for bias: charged words.) Distribute both copies of the piece to opposite sides of the room. Have students analyze the attributes of the president on a web. Then ask them to <u>tell</u> what kind of man they think he was. Using the webs, analyze for bias.

The President achieved notoriety by stubbornly, bitterly, and fanatically asserting his impudent pretensions even in legislative councils, through his tools who cunningly situated themselves on those councils. The Senate being in accord with his prejudices succumbed to his domination. He was a man of superstition and obstinancy whose policy combined bigotry and arrogance with cowardice.

He was a creature of strong biases and belonged in the camp of the reactionaries. His conduct of the presidency portended a degeneration of that office into one of dictatorship.

The President achieved fame by firmly, steadfastly, and gallantly presenting his insightful plans even in legislative councils through his colleagues who honorably seated themselves into those councils. The Senate being in accord with his views, supported his leadership. He was a man of foresight and integrity whose policy combined justice and confidence with courage.

He was a man of conviction and belonged in the league of visionaries. His portrayal of the presidency projected an elevation of that office into one of dignity.

<u>Focus</u>: Distribute the two versions to groups of students on opposite sides of the room without revealing differences. Have them do an attribute web from the readings. Post webs and discuss different profiles and possible points of view represented.

Be aware of point-of-view from title, source, etc.
Indicate bias clues: **EOIOC**
Account for possible bias (i.e.: charged words)
State opinion based on ‘reasoned judgment’

INDEX : Suggested Applications:

MATH:
- Graphs (Possible distortions)
- Perspectives
- Optical Illusions
- Evolution vs. Creation

LANGUAGE ARTS:
- Journalism
- Characters in a Novel

SCIENCE:
- Off-shore Oil Drilling
- Environmental Issues
- Statistics

SOCIAL STUDIES:
- Current Events: Summit Meeting
- Civil War (South/North)
- Industrial Park ⎱
- Super Highway ⎰ Community Issues

51

ANALYZING FOR ASSUMPTION

A SSUME ASSUMPTIONS ARE PRESENT

S EARCH FOR UNSTATED ASSUMPTIONS

S ENSE GAPS

U SE LINKING STATEMENTS

M AKE NECESSARY REVISION

E XPRESS REVISED STATEMENT

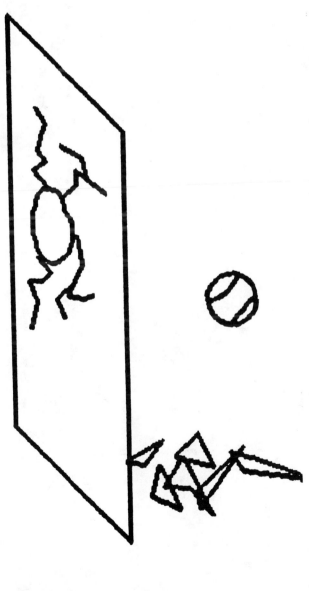

ANALYZING FOR ASSUMPTION

☐ Creative Thinking   ☒ Critical Thinking

PROGRAM : Skill: Analyzing for Assumption   **PASSWORD** : Acronym: **ASSUME**

DATA BASE : Definition: Unwarranted claims; take for granted; broad assertion; generalization that is not stated explicitly.

LIST : Synonyms: take for granted; unstated premise; unwarranted assertions

SCAN : Examples: (1) Claim: Metacognitive thinking is an intelligent behavior.
Assumption: Know what Metacognitive thinking is.

(2) Claim: Economy size.
Assumption: Assume large size will be economic.

ENTER : When to use:
— analyzing information from media sources
— analyzing contractual agreements
— negotiating a position

MENU : How to use:
Assume assumptions are present
Search deliberately for unstated assumptions
Sense gaps between conclusion and premise
Use linking statements to validate or invalidate
Make necessary revision to clarify position
Express revised statement

DEBUGGING : What to do if:
— assumption is spotted; articulate unstated assumptions; clarify.
— assumption is invalid; clarify and restate position.

VISUAL LAYOUT : Patterns: Narrative

Logic: so, thus, therefore, without

Discussion

FILE : Sample Lesson:

Social Studies: Geographic Population Shifts

Statement: Many people are moving to the South and Southwest because they have more money today than in past generations.

Assume assumption present: What assumptions are present?

Search: Is the reason why people are moving south monetary?

Sense gaps: other factors might be that there are more older people; there are people who like warm climate.

Use linking statements: People are moving south; <u>therefore</u> there are reasons. People moving south are often retired; thus, they have a fixed income.

Make revisions: Perhaps the reason people are moving to the South and Southwest is because they want to retire in warmer climates.

Express revised statement: Many people moving to the South and Southwest are retirees who desire warmer climates and can afford the move.

INDEX : Suggested Applications:

<u>MATH</u>:
- Assumptions on: Correctness of Data: Statistics, Stocks, Previous Knowledge

<u>LANGUAGE ARTS</u>:
- Character Analysis
- Hidden Agenda
- Author's Intent
- Assume Others Know

<u>SCIENCE</u>:
- Space Program: Assume Public and Political Support
- USSR: Assume <u>They</u> Too Want Peace
   Assume <u>They</u> Too Are Reasonable

<u>SOCIAL STUDIES</u>:
- Economic Policy
- Political Positions
- Geographic Population Shifts

SOLVING ANALOGIES

S TATE MEANING

O FFER POSSIBLE RELATIONSHIP

L OOK FOR SIMILAR RELATIONSHIP

V ERIFY WITH A CONNECTOR

E XPRESS BEST ANSWER

SOLVING ANALOGIES

☐ Creative Thinking   ☒ Critical Thinking

PROGRAM : Skill: Solving Analogies

PASSWORD : Acronym: **SOLVE**

DATA BASE : Definition: Inferring a relationship and mapping a similar relationship to converge on the best answer.

LIST : Synonyms: metaphors, similes, verbal equations, concrete mapped relationships

SCAN : Examples: Washington : 1 : : Lincoln : 5 (3, 5, 8, 9)
car : transportation : : telephone : communication

ENTER : When to use:
— to test relationships
— to describe an abstract idea
— to state or define relationships

MENU : How to use:

State meaning

Offer possible relationship suggested in 1st part

Look for similar relationship in 2nd part and map same relationship from 1st part to 2nd part

Verify with a verbal connector

Express best answer

DEBUGGING : What to do if:
— it doesn't fit, go back to step one.
— two fit, use a verbal connector to check for consistency.

FILE : Sample Lesson:

Science: Biology — Relationships

INPUT: ANALOGY MODELS

The following examples of analogies set forth a number of the more common relationships customarily found in analogies that are given in a typical aptitude test.

1. CAUSE is to its EFFECT.
   Example: PROSPERITY : HAPPINESS : : success : joy

2. ONE IMPORTANT PART is to its WHOLE.
   Example: BLADE (cutting part) : KNIFE : : prong : fork

3. The EXTREME of one thing is to the EXTREME of another.
   Example: ELATION : DEPRESSION : : acuteness : dullness

4. An OBJECT is to its PRIMARY FUNCTION.
   Example: STOKER : HEAT: : lamp : light

5. A SPECIFIC ITEM is to its GENERAL CLASS.
   Example: CRAB: CRUSTACEAN : : man : mammal

6. An OBJECT is to its CHARACTERISTIC.
   Example: IRON : RIGID : : rubber : flexible

7. This WORD is to its SYNONYM.
   Example: LUGUBRIOUS: SAD : : doleful : mournful

8. This WORD is to its ANTONYM.
   Example: DESTITUTE : WEALTHY : : deplete : fill

9. This OBJECT HINDERS this ACTION.
   Example: FETTER : MOVEMENT : : stutter: speech

10. This OBJECT ASSISTS this action.
    Example: VASELINE : BURN : : consolation : grief

11. This OBJECT is COMPOSED of this MATERIAL.
    Example: SHOE : LEATHER : : coat : cloth

12. An OBJECT is to its DEFINITION.
    Example: DOGMATIC : POSITIVE : : provincial : narrow-minded

Focus: (i.e.: _____ : _____ : : _____ : _____)
(is to)   (as)   (is to)

   a. turtle : eggs : : humans : _____
   b. heart: blood : : lungs : _____
   c. plants: CO_2 : : people : _____
   d. penguin : upright : : elephant : _____
   e. grass : photosynthesis : : butterfly : _____

(S) a turtle and egg are the relevant terms to encode; state meanings.

(O) offer idea: relating terms turtle and egg — a turtle lays eggs.

(L) therefore, a human lays? young by giving birth.

(V) Verify with verbal connector:

   A turtle reproduces by laying eggs; a human reproduces by giving live birth.

(E) Express: turtle : eggs : : human : live young

INDEX : Suggested Applications:

MATH:	• Fractions/Decimals
	• Ratios
LANGUAGE ARTS:	• Vocabulary Development
	• Fiction/Non-Fiction (elements)
SCIENCE:	• Earth Science: Insects
	• Physics: Matter
	• Chemistry: Compounds/Reactions
SOCIAL STUDIES:	• Political Ideologies
	• Economics: Terms

EVALUATING

REVIEW CRITERIA

APPLY CRITERIA

TALLY WORTH

EXPRESS JUDGMENT

EVALUATING

☐ Creative Thinking   ☒ Critical Thinking

PROGRAM : Skill: Evaluating   **PASSWORD** : Acronym: **RATE**

DATA BASE : Definition: To judge worth of.

LIST : Synonyms: judge, critique, rate, appraise, assess

SCAN : Examples: Evaluate the 'best buy', judge the results

ENTER : When to use:
  — judging results
  — determining best choice
  — checking solution

MENU : How to use:

  Review criteria
  Apply criteria
  Tally worth
  Express judgment

DEBUGGING : What to do if:
  — two choices appear equal; add to criteria to follow intuition.
  — none seem good; start over.
  — trouble setting criteria; exaggerate to emphasize.

VISUAL LAYOUT : Patterns: Criteria Grid
PNI Chart
Decision Tree
Priority Ladder

FILE : Sample Lesson:

Health — Nutrition: Sugar (Label Reading on Cereals)
Vocabulary: dextrin, dextrose, sucrose, lactose, maltose,
maltodextrin, corn syrup

(1) **R**eview criteria: Best nutritional value that tastes good.

(2) **A**pply criteria:

Breakfast Cereals	"Hidden Sugar"	Nutrition Value	Taste	Cost
Wheaties	4%	?		
Cheerios	4%	?		
Shredded Wheat	0%	+		
Fruit Loops	50%	–		
Sugar Smacks	63%	–		
Grape Nuts	0%	+		
Frosted Flakes	48%	–		

(3) **T**ally: 1st [ ]

(4) **E**xpress judgment of best. 2nd [ ]

INDEX : Suggested Applications:

MATH:
- Consumer Education
- Probabilities
- Stock Market

LANGUAGE ARTS:
- Evaluating Essay Questions
- Preference for Authors
- Public Spending

SCIENCE:
- Environmental Issues
- Space Exploration
- Archeology

SOCIAL STUDIES:
- Pros and Cons of an Argument (Debate)
- Safety Factors (School Rules)
- Law

DECISION MAKING

JOT DOWN OCCASION FOR DECISION

USE BRAINSTORMING FOR ALTERNATIVES

DECIDE ON BEST POSSIBILITIES

GAUGE POSITIVE AAD NEGATIVE OUTCOMES

EXPRESS SELECTION; DECIDE

DECISION MAKING

☐ Creative Thinking   ☒ Critical Thinking

PROGRAM : Skill: Decision Making   **PASSWORD** : Acronym: **JUDGE**

DATA BASE : Definition: Making a choice based on reasoned judgement.

LIST : Synonyms: judging, choosing, selecting

SCAN : Examples: Auto purchase, college selection, career choices, purchasing gifts

ENTER : When to use:
    — When alternatives present themselves
    — rationalizing <u>best</u> of several options
    — justifying plan of action

MENU : How to use:

    Jot down occasion for decision
    Use brainstorming for alternatives
    Decide on best possibilities
    Gauge positive and negative outcomes
    Express selection; decide

DEBUGGING : What to do if:
    — both seem positive — add to criteria; follow "gut" feeling.
    — both seem negative — add to criteria; follow "gut" feeling.
    — cannot decide — seem equal — select by chance — toss a coin.

VISUAL LAYOUT : Patterns: Concept Map
                     Decision-Making Model

FILE : Sample Lesson:

Social Studies: Selecting an Essay Topic About the Civil War

Jot down occasion for decisions "need essay topic on civil war"

Use brainstorming

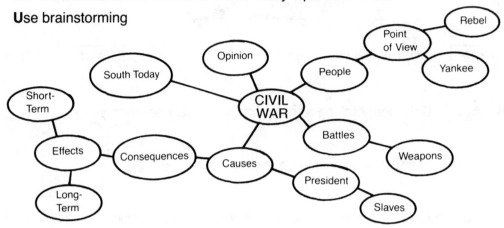

Decide on several alternatives

Gauge positive and negative outcomes

Express selection

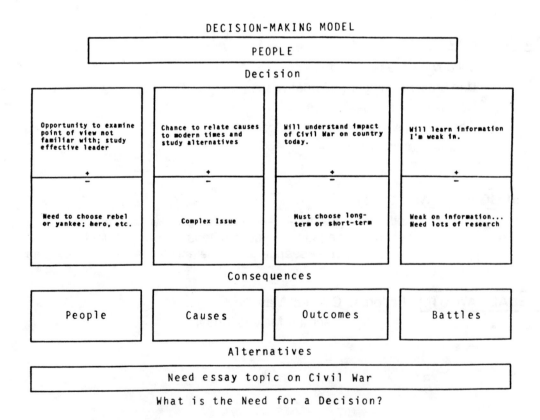

CREATIVE THINKING SKILLS

BRAINSTORMING

TARGET CONCEPT AND START LIST

HITCH-HIKE ON IDEAS; ASSOCIATE

IMAGE; VISUALIZE

NOTE CATEGORIES; ADD MORE

KEEP REVIEWING TO GENERATE MORE

BRAINSTORMING

☒ Creative Thinking   ☐ Critical Thinking

PROGRAM : Skill: Brainstorming   **PASSWORD** : Acronym: **THINK**

DATA BASE : Definition: Generating a fluent list of ideas by associations; idea-finding.

LIST : Synonyms: listing, idea-finding

SCAN : Examples: List of inventions, sports, foods

ENTER : When to use:
— alternative ideas are needed
— looking for a new or improved way

MENU : How to use:

Target concept and start list

Hitch-hike on ideas; associate

Image; visualize

Note categories; add more

Keep reviewing items to generate more connections

DEBUGGING : What to do if:
— running down; look for associations or patterns.
— large quantity of ideas; categorize.
— exhausted ideas; leave it for a time, then go back.
— want more; review list.

VISUAL LAYOUT : Patterns: Concept Map
Clustering
Thought Trees
List
Web

FILE : Sample Lesson:

Science: Birds

Target concept and list; robin, sparrow, wren, ostrich, sea gull, parrot, duck, crow, bluebird, and bluejay.

Hitch-hike; make associations:
duck ⟶ Mallard ⟶ Donald ⟶ Daffy ⟶ geese ⟶ Canadian

Image; visualize: "see" birds in your mind's eye

Note categories: Small-humming
Domestic-chicken
Cartoon-Road Runner
Edible-cornish hen
Exotic-parakeet
Sports Teams-Orioles
Prey-eagle
Color-blackbird

Keep reviewing to generate more; "Bridging or Plugging-In"

INDEX : Suggested Applications:

MATH:
- Terms Used in Measurement
- Tesselations
- Fractions

HISTORY:
- Chinese Contribution to Modern World
- A Democratic Society
- Profiles of Courage

LANGUAGE ARTS:
- Words for Alliterations
- Physical Traits to Develop a Character
- Research Topics for Women in Literature
- Synonyms

SCIENCE:
- The Solar System
- Electricity
- Inventions

VISUALIZING

I MAGINE FINAL GOAL

M ENTALLY PICK A STARTING POINT

A DD, STEP BY STEP TO YOUR FINAL GOAL

G RAPH YOUR STEPS

E LIMINATE POSSIBLE BARRIERS

S EE THE FINAL IMAGED GOAL

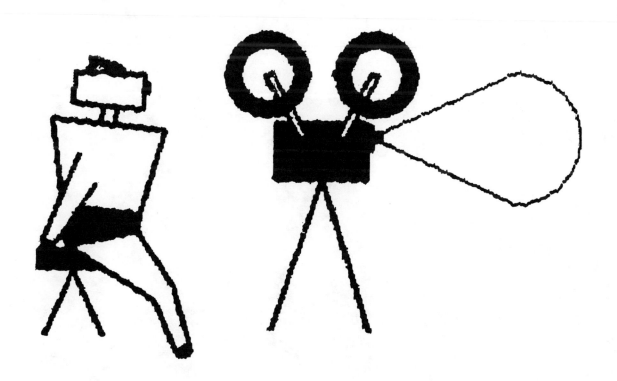

VISUALIZING

[X] Creative Thinking ☐ Critical Thinking

PROGRAM : Skill: Imagining/Visualizing   PASSWORD : Acronym: **IMAGES**

DATA BASE : Definition: Seeing, imagining a picture of an idea or concept; visualizing in the "mind's eye"; mental images.

LIST : Synonyms: imagining, picturing, seeing, imaging

SCAN : Examples: Dreaming, visualizing a place you've visited, imaging yourself winning a race

ENTER : When to use:
 — at the beginning stages of an idea or goal; trying to visualize a final outcome or product

MENU : How to use:
 Imagine final goal
 Mentally pick a starting point
 Add, step by step to your final goal
 Graph your steps
 Eliminate possible barriers
 See the final imaged goal

DEBUGGING : What to do if:
 — cannot see an image, picture "putting it together" using color and all your senses.
 — cannot trace path, leave it; come back later.

VISUAL LAYOUT : Patterns: _____ is like _____ because _____.

FILE : Sample Lesson:

Science: Gravity: Imagine what would happen if gravity stopped for one second every day. Imagine what things would be like. What would land surfaces look like? How about the oceans and the rivers? Create a scenario depicting this concept. (Adapted from Roger Von Oech's, *Whack On The Side Of The Head*.)

Operations:

Imagine the final goal. Using all your senses picture a scene in detail in that one minute of <u>no</u> gravity.

Mentally, go back and pick a starting point. See the same scene <u>with</u> gravity.

Add, step by step to the moment of no gravity. See, in detail, the changes that occur.

Graph your steps mentally until you have a vivid and detailed picture.

Eliminate possible barriers to your mental picture; concentrate on each separate aspect, then pull it together.

See the finished picture of your scene during that one moment of no gravity.

INDEX : Suggested Applications:

MATH:
- Infinity
- The United States as a Communist Society

LANGUAGE ARTS:
- Descriptive Passages
- Characters in a Novel

SCIENCE:
- Pre-Historic Times
- Life on Another Planet
- Sea Community

SOCIAL STUDIES:
- Life in Another Country
- The United States as a Communist Society

PERSONIFYING

Look at object

Imagine actions

Validate with feelings

Express empathetic action

PERSONIFYING

☒ Creative Thinking   ☐ Critical Thinking

PROGRAM : Skill: Personifying   **PASSWORD** : Acronym: **LIVE**

DATA BASE : Definition: Becoming the object; attributing object with life; assuming empathetic action of thing.

LIST : Synonyms: alive, living, becoming

SCAN : Examples:

- Pretend you are a pencil. What do you do and what does it feel like? (action/feelings)
- Michner's writings often use personification; for example in *Centennial*, the sequence depicting the beavers is classic.
- E.B. White personified a spider in his classic: *Charlotte's Web*.

ENTER : When to use:

— trying to imagine or understand from a unique viewpoint
— fantasizing another viewpoint
— trying to understand something more thoroughly
— writing fiction

MENU : How to use:

Look at object and circumstances
Imagine actions
Validate with empathetic feelings
Express empathetic action as you become the thing

DEBUGGING : What to do if:

— cannot imagine actions; hold the object or research it through visual and verbal material; study it.

— cannot visualize or sense feelings; study it more closely; use all senses to imagine feelings.

VISUAL LAYOUT : Patterns: Provide a visual outline for students to use as they write: i.e. :

FILE : Sample Lesson:

Science: Pre-Historic Times

Look at the thing and circumstances: dinosaur
- earth filled with vegetation
- no threats to existence
- other pre-historic animals

Imagine actions: (1) looking for food
(2) other similar animals
(3) home
(4) roaming and wandering

Validate with feelings: lonely   lazy
serene content

Express empathetic action: As I wander about in search of tasty tidbits, I keep hoping I will see other moving creatures . . . etc.

INDEX : Suggested Applications:

MATH:
- Become a Cubic Centimeter
- Become a Multiplication Sign (or Square Root Sign, etc.)
- Become a Point on a Cartisian Graph

LANGUAGE
ARTS:
- Become an Exclamation Point
- Become a Character in a Novel
- Become an Adjective (or verb, adverb, etc.)

SCIENCE:
- Become a Shooting Star
- Become a Grain of Sand

SOCIAL
STUDIES:
- Become the Leader of a Country
- Become a Slave
- Become a Stock on the Stock Market

INVENTING

S ubstituting

C ombining

A dapting

M odifying

    M agnifying

    M inifying

P utting to other uses

E liminating

R eversing or rearranging

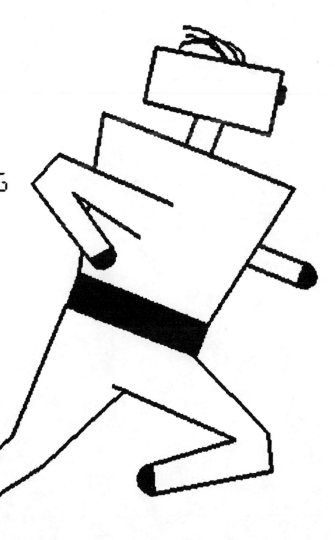

INVENTING

[X] Creative Thinking   [ ] Critical Thinking

PROGRAM : Skill: Inventing   **PASSWORD** : Acronym: **SCAMPER**

DATA BASE : Definition: A deliberate search to generate ideas; a way to visualize alternatives.

LIST : Synonyms: brainstorming, creating, synthesizing, making

SCAN : Examples: Big Clip — magnified; tab diaper — modified; flashback — reversed

ENTER : When to use:
- — spontaneous brainstorm runs down
- — going for vast quantity
- — want to cover all bases

MENU : How to use: Brainstorm first, then try:

Substituting
Combining
Adapting
Modifying
    Magnifying
    Minifying
Putting To Other Uses
Eliminating or Omiting
Reversing or Rearranging

DEBUGGING : What to do if:
- — cannot think of one for one of the methods, go on to the next, then go back.
- — stuck, go on and skip some steps.

VISUAL LAYOUT : Patterns: SCAMPER Chart
Mind Map
Concept Web

FILE : Sample Lesson:

Mathematics: Solving Story Problems

(1) Problem: If everyone in this room shook hands once with every other person in the room, how many handshakes would there be?

(2) Gather facts, discuss, and try it.

(3) **S**ubstitute: Use whole numbers for fractions; use an equation, formula; use smaller numbers.

Combine: Sequence a series of steps to arrive at final solution.

Adapt: Use graph, chart, picture, diagram.

Modify: Round off, estimate, use calculator.

Magnify: Exaggerate to clarify; to check.

Minify: Find smaller problems within.

Put To Other Uses: Associate with similar problems you've solved before; make concrete; do it.

Eliminate: What factors are relevant? What can you omit?

Reverse: Start with end result and work backwards.

Rearrange: Start with what you know, then go to unknown; use manipulatives.

INDEX : Suggested Applications:

MATH: • Discerning Patterns
• Surface Area

LANGUAGE • Biography or Autobiography
ARTS: • Mystery

SCIENCE: • Concept of Motion
• Chemical Bonding

SOCIAL • Supply and Demand
STUDIES: • Equality

ASSOCIATING RELATIONSHIPS

REVIEW THE DATA OR PLOT THE DATA

EXTRACT THE "BIG PICTURE"

LOOK FOR SPECIFICS

ASSOCIATE SPECIFICS BY GROUPING

TEST PATTERN OR RELATIONSHIP

EXPRESS FINDINGS

ASSOCIATING RELATIONSHIPS

[X] Creative Thinking   [ ] Critical Thinking

PROGRAM : Skill: Associating Relationships   **PASSWORD** : Acronym: **RELATE**

DATA BASE : Definition: Seeing patterns; finding relationships; associating ideas; constructing connections; mapping the relationships through reasoning by analogies; seeking structure.

LIST : Synonyms: associating, relating, connecting, perceiving patterns

SCAN : Examples: (1) Discerning patterns from graphs
(2) Reasoning by analogy: Solar Energy as Heat Source
    (a) Sun : Warmth : : Oil : Energy
    (b) Sun : Energy
If the sun provides heat and oil is used to produce energy for heating homes, the sun could be used as a source of energy to heat homes.

ENTER : When to use:
    — to generalize, conclude, or infer through associations
    — to detect a pattern for prediction purposes
    — to extract a trend or probable occurrence

MENU : How to use:

Review the data or plot the data

Extract the "big picture"

Look for specifics

Associate specifics by relating or grouping in some way

Test pattern or relationship

Express findings

DEBUGGING : What to do if:
- cannot find relationship(s); review again by making a visual layout of material.
- see more than one relationship; extract them separately, then pull them together holistically.

VISUAL LAYOUT : Patterns: Analogy Equation Format (__ : __ : : __ : __)
Graphs and Grids

FILE : Sample Lesson:

Math: Graphing — Prime Time T.V. Shows

Review data: Use TV guide to graph <u>types</u> of TV shows aired from 7-9 p.m. for one week.

Extract "Big Picture": Articulate "big picture" or first impression of data.

Look for specifics: Look at specifics by plotting by categories on a graph.

Associate specifics: Try to connect or associate data from graph to audience preference.

Test pattern: Survey some people to test ideas.

Express findings: Tell the relationship(s) you found.

INDEX : Suggested Applications:

<u>MATH</u>:
- Sequences
- Graphs
- Geometry
- Computer Graphics
- Architecture and Culture

<u>LANGUAGE</u> <u>ARTS</u>:
- TV
- Poetry
- Soap Operas
- Commercials
> Patterns

<u>SCIENCE</u>:
- Reaction Patterns: Chemistry
- Patterns in Nature

<u>SOCIAL</u> <u>STUDIES</u>:
- Reaction Patterns
- Associating Relationships

INFERRING

Identify literal interpretation

Note indicators of further meaning

Find evidence of subtle clues

Extend original interpretation

Restate revised interpretation

INFERRING

☒ Creative Thinking   ☐ Critical Thinking

PROGRAM : Skill: Inferring   **PASSWORD** : Acronym: **INFER**

DATA BASE : Definition: Making an assumption based on subtle, verbal, and non-verbal clues; 'reading between the lines'; assuming; deducing from indications; and drawing conclusions.

LIST : Synonyms: assume, deduce, imply

SCAN : Examples: Infer moods from facial clues, body language, tone of voice

ENTER : When to use:
— looking beyond the literal; sensing moods, evaluating point of view, propaganda, advertising, and political messages.

MENU : How to use:

Identify literal, face-value interpretation

Note indicators of further meaning, verbal and non-verbal clues that suggest possible variances or confirmations of the literal interpretation (what else is there?)

Find evidence of subtle clues; analyze the nuances and indicators

Extend original interpretation based on inferences made from the 'hidden' clues

Restate revised interpretation

DEBUGGING : What to do if:
— cannot infer beyond literal, discuss with someone else and compare. be sensitive to your intuition, let your internal radar guide you to inferences.

VISUAL LAYOUT : Patterns:

Charts

| 1st Level — Interpretation |
| 2nd Level — Inferences |
| 3rd Level — Conclusion |

: Sample Lesson:

English

<u>Concept</u>: Critical Reading

Do you or your loved ones ever have any trouble with the problem of worry, fear, or anxiety? Do you get discouraged or depressed, and even lack faith in yourself? Does an inferiority complex ever plague you? Do you ever feel resentful, or do bad relations ever develop between you and other people?

There is an answer to all such human problems, and it's an answer that works. It is to develop the process or right thinking and a faith that lifts you above defeat.

I believe we have something that can be of help to you and those whom you love. Right off, let me say we are not selling anything — just offering something that can bring new happiness to you.

And it is this: For many years I have talked every Sunday at my church on Fifth Avenue at 29th Street in New York City to large audiences on the above-mentioned matters and kindred subjects. There grew a demand to have these talks, all of which dealt with practical, workable methods for happy and successful living, made available in printed form. One-half million people are receiving three of these practical guides to living each month and the total readership is several million.

<u>Operations</u>:

Identify literal interpretation.
There <u>is</u> an answer to human problems of worry, fear, anxiety, and depression.

Note indicators of further meaning — questions asked in the article, possible answer(s), and others.

Find evidence of subtle clues.
"I believe we have someting for you."
"Not selling anything."
"Available in printed form."
"Half million people receiving . . . practical guides."

Extend original interpretation based on clues.
Possibly selling something based on protest of <u>not</u> selling and then going on to tell what <u>is</u> available.

Restate revised interpretation based on inferences.
The author is appealing to the aspect of human nature in all of us that seeks happiness and solutions to our problems. He or she is probably "selling" something— so the reader should be cognizant of that while reading the piece.

INDEX : Suggested Applications:

MATH:
- Problem Solving
- Patterns

LANGUAGE
ARTS:
- Poetry
- Drama: Inferring Mood (actions/facial expressions/tone)

SCIENCE:
- Chemical Compounds
- Friction
- Medical Diagnosis

SOCIAL
STUDIES:
- Political Speeches
- Consumer Education
- Government Policy

GENERALIZING

Round up specific data

Uncover patterns

Label all rules

Evaluate validity

GENERALIZING

[X] Creative Thinking   [ ] Critical Thinking

PROGRAM : Skill: Generalizing   **PASSWORD** : Acronym: **RULE**

DATA BASE : Definition: A broad statement; summary of information material into a rule.

LIST : Synonyms: summary, all encompassing statement, rule

SCAN : Examples: <u>Megatrends</u> — looking at trends from newspaper clippings to make
generalizations about the future

ENTER : <u>When to use:</u>
   — have a smattering of facts; looking for pattern
   — several occurrences indicate generalized trend

MENU : <u>How to use:</u>

   Round up specific data
   Uncover patterns
   Label all encompassing rules
   Evaluate validity of generalization

DEBUGGING : <u>What to do if:</u>
   — facts seem contradictory; do further testing or get more information.
   — cannot see pattern; leave and come back or continue with data collection.

VISUAL LAYOUT : Patterns: Venn Diagram
                          Chart
                          Matrix

FILE : Sample Lesson:

Language Arts: Newspapers and Magazines
                 Trend Analysis

Round up data: Gather information on fashions or automobile models; collect pictures and articles from many sources.

Uncover patterns; look for similarities in fashion designs and auto styles and models.

Label trends evidenced by patterns of similarities in fashions or autos. (i.e. skirt lengths shorter; "box" jackets, contrasting primary colors-indicate fashion trend.)

Evaluate validity of generalization

Example: Fashion

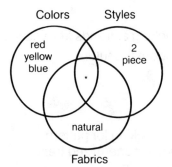

*style emerging

INDEX : Suggested Applications:

MATH: • Discerning Patterns
             • Statistics
             • Stocks and Bonds

LANGUAGE   • Writer's Style
ARTS: • Periods of Literature
             • Changes in Language (Word Usage)

SOCIAL   • Economic Trends
STUDIES: • Import/Export
             • Political Climate
             • Cultures

SCIENCE: • Environmental Issues
             • Inductive Reasoning — Lab Experiments

PREDICTING

BASE ON FACTS

EXPRESS PROBABILITIES AND POSSIBILITIES

TENDER YOUR BET; TAKE A GUESS

PREDICTING

☒ Creative Thinking   ☐ Critical Thinking

PROGRAM : Skill: Predicting   **PASSWORD** : Acronym: **BET**

DATA BASE : Definition: Anticipating what comes next.

LIST : Synonyms: forecasting, guessing, anticipating

SCAN : Examples: Predicting weather, trends, outcomes

ENTER : <u>When to use:</u>
    — for focused, attentive reading
    — in experiments
    — in anticipating outcomes of decisions

MENU : <u>How to use:</u>

    Base on facts

    Examine probabilities and possibilities from clues

    Tender your bet; take a guess

DEBUGGING : <u>What to do if:</u>
    — cannot find obvious clues, infer from feelings, tone, sensing; or intuition.
    — guessing wrong; keep trying.

VISUAL LAYOUT : Patterns: Chart

Literature: "The Dinner Party" by Mona Gardner (Predicting)

THE DINNER PARTY
by Mona Gardner

The country is India. A colonial official and his wife are giving a large dinner party. They are seated with their guests — army officers and government attaches and their wives, and a visiting American naturalist — in their spacious dining room, which has a bare marble floor, open rafters, and wide glass doors opening onto a veranda.

A spirited discussion springs up between a young girl who insists that women have outgrown the jumping-on-a-chair-at-the-sight-of-a-mouse era and a colonel who says that they haven't.

"A woman's unfailing reaction in any crisis," the colonel says, "is to scream. And while a man may feel like it, he has that ounce more of nerve control than a woman has. And that last ounce is what counts."

The American does not join in the argument but watches the other guests. As he looks, he sees a strange expression come over the face of the hostess. She is staring straight ahead, her muscles contracting slightly. With a slight gesture she summons the native boy standing behind her chair and whispers to him. The boy's eyes widen, and he quickly leaves the room.

Of the guests, none except the American notices this or sees the boy place a bowl of milk on the veranda just outside the open doors.

The American comes to with a start. In India, milk in a bowl means only one thing — bait for a snake. He realizes there must be a cobra in the room. He looks up at the rafters — the likeliest place — but they are bare. Three corners of the room are empty, and in the fourth the servants are waiting to serve the next course. There is only one place left — under the table.

His first impulse is to jump back and warn the others, but he knows the commotion would frighten the cobra into striking. He speaks quickly, the tone of his voice so arresting that it sobers everyone.

"I want to know just what control everyone at this table has. I will count three hundred — that's five minutes — and not one of you is to move a muscle. Those who move will forfeit fifty rupees. Ready!"

The twenty people sit like stone images while he counts. He is saying ". . . two hundred and eighty . . ." when, out of the corner of his eye, he sees the cobra emerge and make for the bowl of milk. Screams ring out as he jumps to slam the veranda doors safely shut.

"You were right, Colonel" the host exclaims. "A man has just shown us an example of perfect control."

"Just a minute," the American says, turning to his hostess. "Mrs. Wynnes, how did you know that cobra was in the room?"

A faint smile lights up the woman's face as she replies: "Because it was crawling across my foot."

"The Dinner Party" by Mona Gardner,
Saturday Review, January 31, 1942.

Focus: — Gather facts by reading 1st paragraph.
— Look for clues to possible or probable outcomes.
— Guess, based on your clues.
— Prove by stating clues (or reading to verify)
— Repeat "BET" throughout the piece.

> **B**ase on fact
> **E**xamine possibilities
> **T**ender your bet

INDEX : Suggested Applications:

MATH: • Probabilities
• Estimations
• Stock Market

LANGUAGE • Short Stories — Predict Endings
ARTS: • Write a Scenario of the Future
• Have Students Predict Their Future Careers and Support Prediction

SCIENCE: • Weather Predictions
• Predict the Next Breakthrough in Medicine
• Predict Changes in Physiology that We Might Expect in the Future
• Lab Experiments

SOCIAL • "Turning Points" in History (What if . . .)
STUDIES: • Current Events: International Event —Predict Actions and Outcomes
• Prepare a Newscast for the Year 2000

HYPOTHESIZING

T ALLY THE FACTS

H AVE A QUESTION FORMED

E XTRACT RATIONALE AND

O FFER A HYPOTHESIS

R EVIEW BY TESTING HYPOTHESIS

Y IELD PROOF AND STATE HYPOTHESIS

HYPOTHESIZING

☒ Creative Thinking $E = mc^2$ ☐ Critical Thinking

PROGRAM : Skill: Hypothesizing

PASSWORD : Acronym: **THEORY**

DATA BASE : Definition: To assert as or form a theory; to assume subject to verification or proof; a conjecture for a set of facts that can be used as a basis for further investigation.

LIST : Synonyms: postulate, suppose, theorize, conjecture

SCAN : Examples: Hypothesizing in scientific experiments: Why heat rises; forming a theory that warrants further research: Why good readers are good spellers; a conjecture that needs proving: Do other planets support living things?

ENTER : When to use:
— questioning phenomena; trying to articulate the meaning of something to establish a basis for further investigations
— trying to find a rationale or reason for something

MENU : How to use:

Tally the facts as you gather the data

Have a question formed

Extract rationale or a reasonable answer and

Offer a hypothesis or a theory

Review by testing hypothesis

Yield proof and state hypothesis

DEBUGGING : What to do if:
— cannot prove hypothesis; continue testing to find supporting data or revise hypothesis.
— cannot prove hypothesis in <u>every</u> case; continue testing to isolate factors that cause exceptions, restate.
— contradictory facts appear; review and restate hypothesis.

VISUAL LAYOUT : Patterns: Questions
                             Logic
                             Deductive Reasoning

FILE : Sample Lesson:

Science: Psycho-Motor Abilities

Tally facts: After time away from a sport with <u>no</u> practice, such as skiing, one seems to improve in the skill.

Have question: Why do psycho-motor abilities seem to be enhanced by time away from the sport?

Extract rationale: Movements of skiing are learned cognitively first and then become internalized automatically as psycho-motor responses.

Offer theory: After basic and intense practice at a skill, "incubation" time allows the body and mind to meld so that when skill is resumed, reactions have been internalized.

Yield proof and state: After a winter of skiing and summer off, 4 out of 5 students were placed in a higher skill group the following season.

INDEX : Suggested Applications:

MATH:
• Results or Outcomes of Survey
• Statistical Findings

LANGUAGE ARTS:
• Author's Purpose in Writing
• Audience Response to Piece

SCIENCE:
• Experiments with Matter
• Experiments with Energy

SOCIAL STUDIES:
• Hypothesize Why: Government Policies
                              Terrorist Activities

MAKING ANALOGIES

Make a comparison

Acknowledge the similarities

Keep the similarities and <u>infer</u> a relationship

Express the relationship as a metaphor

MAKING ANALOGIES

$\boxed{X}$ Creative Thinking $\boxed{}$ Critical Thinking

$\boxed{\textbf{PROGRAM}}$: Skill: Making Analogies $\boxed{\textbf{PASSWORD}}$: Acronym: **MAKE**

$\boxed{\textbf{DATA BASE}}$: Definition: Creating metaphors to visualize an idea.

$\boxed{\textbf{LIST}}$: Synonyms: metaphors, similes

$\boxed{\textbf{SCAN}}$: Examples: Reasoning by analogy to make abstract concept more concrete;
           rage as thunder, sun as love

$\boxed{\textbf{ENTER}}$: When to use:
           — to grasp abstract concepts
           — to present ideas in unique ways
           — to communicate a complex thought

$\boxed{\textbf{MENU}}$: How to use:

           Make a comparison of two unlike things
           Acknowledge the similarities
           Keep the similarities in mind and infer a relationship
           Express the relationship as a metaphorical image

$\boxed{\textbf{DEBUGGING}}$: What to do if:
           — cannot find similarities; keep brainstorming using all your senses or
             change comparison.

$\boxed{\textbf{VISUAL LAYOUT}}$: Patterns: Thought Trees
                   _____ is like _____ because both _____.

117

FILE : Sample Lesson:

History — Courageous People From History: (Courage)

Focus

Make a comparison: courage and rain.

Acknowledge similarities: both can appear unexpectedly.

Keep similarities in mind and infer a relationship: courage appears like a sudden summer shower — out of nowhere.

Express the relationship as a metaphorical image: courage, like a summer shower, often appears quite unexpectedly.

INDEX : Suggested Applications:

MATH:
- Figural Analogies
- Numerical Analogies
- Concepts of: Fractions   Measurement
                     Decimals   Geometric Shapes

LANGUAGE ARTS:
- Concepts of:

Love	Humor	Grief
Loneliness	Anger	Equality
Isolation	Joy	Sanity

SCIENCE:
- Concepts of:

Smoking	Evolution
Gravity	Electricity
Magnetism	Space Exploration

SOCIAL STUDIES:
- Concepts of:

War	Diplomacy
Poverty	Geographic Locations
Capitalism	Events

DEALING WITH AMBIGUITY AND PARADOX

D ISCUSS CONTRADICTIONS

U SE PLUSES AND MINUSES

A PPROACH FROM BOTH POINTS OF VIEW

L OOK AT YOUR FINAL POSITION

DEALING WITH AMBIGUITY & PARADOX

[X] Creative Thinking  [ ] Critical Thinking

PROGRAM : Skill: Dealing With
Ambiguity and Paradox

PASSWORD : Acronym: **DUAL**

DATA BASE : Definition: Apparent conflicting nature of some things; seeming opposition;
contradictions.

LIST : Synonyms: irony; opposites, contradictions, puzzle, bittersweet situation

SCAN : Examples: (A) <u>Irony</u>: (1) Atomic bomb was a scientific breakthrough for humanity but
could cause <u>end</u> of human race.

(2) Teacher <u>yells</u>, "Be quiet!"

(B) <u>Paradoxical situation</u>: Coward takes action that makes him a hero;
murder out of love.

(C) <u>Ambiguous</u>: Abortion: Personal human rights of mother may be
in conflict with personal human rights of
unborn baby.

ENTER : <u>When to use</u>:

— ambiguous issue; situations that appear contradictory
— "twist" is desired in writing (a la Alfred Hitchcock, O'Henry, etc.)

MENU : <u>How to use</u>:

Discuss contradictions
Use a written format to plot pluses and minuses you attribute to both aspects of the idea
Approach from both points of view or assume both postures to examine thoroughly
Look at your final position on the issue and articulate it with supporting facts

DEBUGGING : <u>What to do if</u>:

— cannot separate the contradictions or seem to be into a circular reasoning
mode; take time to write down points; do more research; examine bias
you may have.

VISUAL LAYOUT : Patterns: Thought Tree
Attribute Web
Attribute Listing
Analogies

FILE : Sample Lesson:

Language Arts: Poetry

Discuss contractions: (a) tears of joy, cruel laughter, joyful regret, peaceful war, honest lie, silent shout, painful pleasure, useful nuisance, deafening silence
(b) How can you tell an honest lie? How can loyal men become traitors? How can you begin without ending? How can you know without knowing?

Use format to attribute both aspects of paradox:

ATTRIBUTE LIST

tears	joy
sad	happy
touched	appreciated
emotional	emotional
reaction	reaction
intense	intense

Approach from both points of view: can be so sad you cry
can be so happy you cry

Look at final position: Grandma was so touched by the photograph of Grandpa, she cried tears of joy.

INDEX : Suggested Applications:

MATH:
• Mobius Strip
• Topography
• Optical Illusions (Escher drawings)

LANGUAGE • (1) *Catch 22:* Paradoxical statements
ARTS: Ambiguous statements in literature
        (2) Irony in Writing

SCIENCE:
• Cancer Treatment
• Life Cycle — (Decay helps create life)

SOCIAL   • Philosophy: Is There More Wisdom In Innocence or Experience?
STUDIES: • Historical Incidents: (Ironic) We Have Defense Build-up To
                                Maintain Peace

PROBLEM SOLVING

INDEX THE FACTS

DEFINE THE PROBLEM

EXPAND ON ALTERNATIVES

ADOPT A CRITERIA; AND

SELECT AND "SELL" YOUR IDEA

PROBLEM SOLVING

X Creative Thinking   ☐ Critical Thinking

PROGRAM : Skill: Problem Solving   **PASSWORD** : Acronym: **IDEAS**

DATA BASE : Definition: Finding alternatives to a situation or circumstance; generating ideas to happening; anticipating a need and examining options.

LIST : Synonyms: trouble shooting, debugging, finding options

SCAN : Examples: Problems:
- You are late for class frequently.
- You want a new bike.
- You need a job.
- You have trouble meeting new people.

ENTER : When to use:

— in a spot
— emergencies
— change is indicated
— anticipating situation

MENU : How to use:

Index the facts as you see them
Define the problem
Expand on ideas or possible alternatives
Adopt a criteria; and
Select and "sell" your idea to others involved

DEBUGGING : What to do if:

— cannot define problem; group facts in some way; write several problems indicated; prioritize; take one at a time.
— cannot think of appropriate alternatives; continue brainstorming; leave alone for a time; ask for help.
— cannot get others to "buy it"; find out what "they" want; modify it; compromise.

VISUAL LAYOUT : Patterns: Problem-Solving Chart
Lists
Clusters

FILE : Sample Lesson:

Social Studies: Family — Privacy: Share bedroom with younger sibling.

Index the facts: lack of privacy affecting school work and "social" life (phone);
one bedroom for 2 of you; some space available in basement;
parents unsympathetic, etc.

Define problem: want more privacy

Expand ideas or alternatives: find another space; divide room; schedule some private time
for each for use of the room; live with it!

Adapt a criteria: expense must be minimal; need parental approval.

Select and "sell" idea: will convert part of basement to "study"; will do all work and pay for
phone installation; will continue to <u>sleep</u> in bedroom with sibling.

INDEX : Suggested Applications:

MATH: • Architectual Plans
• Economic Issues (Budgets, etc.)

LANGUAGE • Conflict Resolutions in Literature
ARTS: • Word Usage and Choices

SCIENCE: • Medical Dilemmas
• Environmental Issues
• Energy Sources
• Car Breaks Down

SOCIAL   Simulations on:
STUDIES: (1) Space Exploration
(2) World War II
(3) Social Issues: Indian Reservations
Slums
Etc.

APPENDIX

Possible Subject Area Clusters For Thinking Skills

SUBJECT AREA	THINKING SKILLS	
READING	Visualizing Predicting Analyzing for Bias	Generalizing Inferring Sequencing
WRITING	Brainstorming Inventing Personifying	Making Analogies Analyzing for Assumption Problem Solving
MATH	Predicting Associating Relationships Inventing	Solving Analogies Problem Solving Evaluating
SOCIAL STUDIES	Determining Cause/Effect Dealing w/Ambiguity-Paradox Generalizing	Decision Making Comparing and Contrasting Prioritizing
SCIENCE	Hypothesizing Determining Cause/Effect Drawing Conclusions	Attributing Classifying Evaluating
PRACTICAL ARTS (PE/Music/Art Business/Home & Industrial)	Visualizing Brainstorming Sequencing	Inventing Problem Solving Decision Making

References

Ainsworth-Land, Vaune and Fletcher, Norma. *Making Waves with Creative Problem-Solving.* D.O.K. Publishers, Inc., New York, 1979.

Alexander, Cynthia and Cowell, Juliette. *Mapping Insights.* Learning Insights, 1983.

Bellanca, James. *Skills For Critical Thinking.* Illinois Renewal Institute, Inc., 1984.

Bellanca, James; Fogarty, Robin; and Opeka, Kay. IRI, Inc. *Patterns For Thinking,* 2d Edition. 1985.

Bellanca, James and Fogarty, Robin. *Planning For Thinking.* IRI, Inc. 1986.

Bellanca, James and Fogarty, Robin. *Catch Them Thinking. A Handbook of Classroom Strategies.* IRI, Inc., April, 1986

Beyer, Berry. "Common Sense About Teaching Thinking Skills," *EDUCATIONAL LEADERSHIP.* November 1984, pp. 57-62.

Beyer, Berry. "Improving Thinking Skills — Defining the Problem," *PHI DELTA KAPPAN.* March 1984, pp. 486-490.

Biondi, A. (ed.) *The Creative Process.* Creative Education Foundation, Inc., D.O.K. Publishers, Inc., 1972.

Black, Howard & Sandra. *Figural Analogies.* Midwest Publications, CA 93950.

Bloom, Benjamin. *All Our Children Learning. A Primer For Parents, Teachers, and Educators.* McGraw-Hill Book Company, London, 1981.

Bloom, Benjamin S. (Ed.) *Taxonomy of Educational Objectives: Cognitive Domain.* New York, David McKay Company, Inc., 1956.

Burns, Marilyn. *The Book of Think or How to Solve a Problem Twice Your Size.* Little, Brown & Company, Boston, 1976.

Carpenter, E.T. (1980). Piagetian Interviews of college students. R.G. Fuller, et al. (Eds.), *Piagetian Programs in Higher Education.* Lincoln, NE: ADAPT, University of Nebraska-Lincoln, 1980, pp. 15-21.

Carpenter, T.P., Corbitt, M.K., Kepner, H., Lindquist, M.M., & Reys, R.W. (1980). "Problem Solving In Mathematics: National Assessment Results." *Educational Leadership, 37,* 562-563.

Clark, Barbara. *Growing Up Gifted.* Charles E. Merrill, 1983.

Clement, J. (1982a). "Algebra Word Problem Solutions: Thought Processes Underlying A Common Misconception." *Journal for Research in Mathematics Education, 13,* 16-30.

Clement, J. (1982b). "Students' Preconceptions In Introductory Mechanics." *American Journal of Physics, 50,* 66-71.

Convigtona, M.V., Crutchfield, R.S., Davies, L., & Olton, R.M. (1974). *The productive thinking program: A course in learning to think.* Columbus, OH: Merill.

Costa, Arthur. (ed.) *Developing Minds,* Alexandria, VA: ASCD, 1985.

Costa, Arthur L. "Mediating the Metacognitive," *EDUCATIONAL LEADERSHIP.* November 1984, pp. 57-62.

Costa, Arthur L. "Teaching For Intelligent Behavior," *EDUCATIONAL LEADERSHIP.* October 1981, pp. 29-32.

Eberle, Bob and Stanish, Bob. *CPS For Kids.* D.O.K., Buffalo, NY, 1980.

Eberle, Robert F. *SCAMPER Games For Imagination Development.* Buffalo, D.O.K. Publishers, 1971.

Eberle, Bob. *Visual Thinking.* D.O.K. Publishers, Buffalo, NY, 1982.

Edwards, Betty. *Drawing On The Right Side of The Brain.* J.P. Tarcher, Inc., Los Angeles, 1979.

Eggen, Kauchak, Harder. *Strategies For Teachers.* Prentice-Hall, 1979.

Elbow, Peter. *Writing Without Teachers.* Oxford University Press, NY, 1973.

Ferguson, Marilyn. *The Aquarian Conspiracy.* J.P. Tarcher, Inc., NY, 1980.

Ferguson, Marilyn. *The Aquarian Conspiracy.* J.P. Tarcher, Inc., NY, 1980.

Gallagher, James J. *Teaching The Gifted Child.* Allyn & Bacon, 1975.

Gallelli, Gene. *Activity Mindset Guide.* D.O.K. Publishers, Inc., NY 1977.

Gardner et al. National Commission on Excellence in Education (1983). *A Nation At Risk: The Imperative for Educational Reform.* Washington, DC: Department of Education.

Good, Thomas. "Teacher Expectations & Student Perceptions." *EDUCATIONAL LEADERSHIP.* February, 1981.

Gordon, W.J.J., and Tony Pose. *Activities in Metaphor.* Porpoise Books, Cambridge, Massachusetts.

Gordon, W.J.J., and Tony Pose. *Teaching is Listening.* Porpoise Books, Cambridge, Massachusetts.

Gordon, Wm. J. *Synectics: The Development of Creative Capacity.* 1968 pap.1.25 (00825, Collier) Macmillan.

Guilford, J.P. *Way Beyond The I.Q.* Creative Education Foundation, Buffalo, NY, 1975.

Harnadek, Anita. *Basic Thinking Skills, Analogies-D.* Midwest Publications Company, Inc., 1977.

Harnadek, Anita. *Critical Thinking,* Midwest Publications, P.O. Box 448, Pacific Grove, CA 93950.

Harnadek, Anita. *Basic Thinking Skills, Patterns.* Midwest Publications, Inc., CA, 1977.

Johnson, Roger & Johnson, David. *Learning Together & Alone.*

Johnson, Roger & Johnson, David. *Circles of Learning.* ASCD, Alexandria, 1984.

Karplus, R. (1974). *Science Curriculum Improvement Study Teachers Handbook,* Berkeley, CA: University of California, Berkeley.

Larkin, J.H., McDermott, J., Simon, D.P., & Simon, H.A. (1980). "Expert and Novice Performance In Solving Physics Problems." *Science, 208,* 1335-1342.

Maraviglia, Christie. *Creative Problem-Solving Think Book.* D.O.K. Publications, Inc., 1978.

McCloskey, M., Carmazza, A., & Green, B. (1980). "Curvilinear Motion in the Absence of External Forces: Naive Beliefs About the Motion of Objects." *Science. 210.* 1130-1141.

Nickerson, R.S. (1982). *Understanding Understanding,* (BBN Report No. 5087).

Nickerson, R.S. (1983). "Computer Programming As A Vehicle for Teaching Thinking Skills." *Journal of Philosophy for Children, 4* (3 & 4).

Nickerson, R.S., Perkins, D.N., & Smith, E.E. (1984). *Teaching Thinking,* (BBN Report No. 5575).

Nickerson, R.S., Salter, W., Shepard, & Herrnstein, J. (1984). *The Teaching of Learning Strategies,* (BBN Report 5578).

Nisbett, R., & Ross, L. (1980). *Human Inference: Strategies and Shortcomings of Social Judgment.* Englewood Cliffs, N.J: Prentice-Hall.

Noller, R., Parnes, S., & Biondi, A. *Creative Action Book.* New York: Scribner's, 1976.

Noller, R., Treffinger, D., and Houseman, E. *It's A Gas To Be Gifted* or *CPS For The Gifted and Talented.* D.O.K. Publishers, Inc., Buffalo, NY, 1979.

Noller, Ruth. *Scratching The Surface of Creative Problem-Solving:* A Bird's Eye View of CPS. D.O.K. Publishers, Inc., Buffalo, NY, 1977.

Osborn, Alex F. *Applied Imagination.* Charles Scribner & Sons, 1979.

Parnes, Sidney. *Aha! Insights Into Creative Behavior.* D.O.K. Publishers, Inc., Buffalo, NY, 1975.

Parnes, Sidney. *Creativity: Unlocking Human Potential.* D.O.K. Publishers, Inc., Buffalo, NY, 1972.

Pearson, Craig. "Can You Keep Quiet for Three Minutes", *Learning,* Palo Alto, February, 1980.

Peters, T. and Austin, N. *Passion For Excellence.* Random House, Inc., NY, 1985.

Peters, T. and Waterman, R., Jr. *In Search of Excellence.* Warner Communication Company, NY, 1982.

Polette, Nancy. *Exploring Books For Gifted Programs.* Scarecrow Press, 1981.

Problem Cards: Attribute Games and Problems. Webster Division: McGraw-Hill Book Company, NY, 1966. (ESS Science Series)

Raths, Louis. *Teaching For Thinking.* Merrill, 1967.

Rico, Gabriele L. *Writing The Natural Way.* J.P. Tarcher, Inc., Boston, 1983.

Rowe, Mary Budd. "Science, Silence and Sanctions," *Science & Children.* 6: 11-13, 1969.

Scardamalia, M., Bereiter, C., & Fillion, B. (1979). *The Little Red Writing Book: A Source Book of Consequential Writing Activities.* Ontario, Canada: Pedagogy of Writing Project, O.I.S.E.

Schoenfeld, A.H. (1980). "Teaching Problem-Solving Skills." *American Mathematical Monthly, 87* (10), 794-805.

Sternberg, Robert J. "Intelligence as Thinking and Learning Skills," *EDUCATIONAL LEADERSHIP.* October, 1981, pp. 18-20.

The College Board (1983). *Academic Preparation for College.* New York, New York.

Torrance, E. Paul. *The Search for Satari and Creativity.* Creative Education Foundation, Buffalo, NY; and Creative Synergetics Associates, Great Neck, NY, 1979.

Tversky, A., Kahneman, D. (1974). "Judgment Under Uncertainty: Heuristics and Biases." *Science, 185,* 1124-1131.

Underwood, V.L. (1982). "Self-management Skills For College Students: A program in how to learn." Unpublished doctoral dissertation, University of Texas.

von Oech, Roger. *A Whack On The Side Of The Head.* New York. Warner Books, Inc., 1983.

Warner, Sylvia Ashton. *Teacher.* Vintage Books, NY, 1972.

Wason, P.C. (1974). "The Psychology of Deceptive Problems." *New Scientist, 63,* 382-385.

Weber, Patricia. *Promote . . . Discovering Ways to Learn and Research.* D.O.K. Publishers, Inc., Buffalo, NY, 1978.

Weber, Patricia. *Question Quest: Discovering Ways to Ask Worthwhile Questions.* D.O.K. Publishers, Inc., Buffalo, NY, 1978.

Weinstein, C.E., Underwood, V.L. (1983). "Learning Strategies: The *How* of Learning." In J. Segal, S. Chipman, & R. Glaser (Eds.) *Relating Instruction To Basic Research.* Hillsdale, N.J.: Lawrence Erlbaum Associates.

Whimbey, Arthur. *Intelligence Can Be Taught.* Innovative Science, Inc., NY, 1975.

Williams, Frank E. *Classroom Ideas For Encouraging Thinking And Feeling.* D.O.K. Publishers, 1970.

Learn from Our Books *and* from Our Authors!

Bring Our Author/Trainers to Your District

At IRI/Skylight, we have assembled a unique team of outstanding author/trainers with international reputations for quality work. Each has designed high-impact programs that translate powerful new research into successful learning strategies for every student. We design each program to fit your school's or district's special needs.

Training Programs

IRI/Skylight's training programs extend the renewal process by helping educators move from content-centered to mind-centered classrooms. In our highly interactive workshops, participants learn foundational, research-based information and teaching strategies in an instructional area that they can immediately transfer to the classroom setting. With IRI/Skylight's specially prepared materials, participants learn how to teach their students to learn for a lifetime.

Network for Systemic Change

Through a partnership with Phi Delta Kappa, IRI/Skylight offers a Network for site-based systemic change: *The Network of Mindful Schools.* The Network is designed to promote systemic school change as possible and practical when starting with a renewed vision that centers on *what* and *how* each student learns. To help accomplish this goal, Network consultants work with member schools to develop an annual tactical plan and then implement that plan at the classroom level.

Training of Trainers

The Training of Trainers programs train your best teachers, those who provide the highest quality instruction, to coach other teachers. This not only increases the number of teachers you can afford to train in each program, but also increases the amount of coaching and follow-up that each teacher can receive from a resident expert. Our Training of Trainers programs will help you make a systemic improvement in your staff development program.

To receive a FREE COPY of the IRI/Skylight catalog or more information about trainings offered through IRI/Skylight, contact CLIENT SERVICES at

TRAINING AND PUBLISHING, INC.
2626 S. Clearbrook Dr., Arlington Heights, IL 60005
800-348-4474 • 847-290-6600 • FAX 847-290-6609

There are
one-story intellects,
two-story intellects, and three-story
intellects with skylights. All fact collectors, who
have no aim beyond their facts, are one-story men. Two-story men
compare, reason, generalize, using the labors of the fact collectors as
well as their own. Three-story men idealize, imagine,
predict—their best illumination comes from
above, through the skylight.
—*Oliver Wendell*
Holmes

IRI SkyLight

TRAINING AND PUBLISHING, INC.